MW01268490

THE
BLACK
MARKET
CONCIERGE

Sanction Busting, Smuggling &
Spying for America

*

By Barry Oberholzer

With Tim Lister

DEDICATION

To Chloe, Claudia-Joy and my wonderful wife, the only one who really knows what we have been through.

****

To war veterans, serving soldiers, intelligence agents and informants in every country and on every continent. Whatever ideologies separate us; we are all human.

Table of Contents

AUTHOR'S NOTE

Any confidential informant, intelligence asset, or agent who goes public will face scrutiny. This book is a work of memoir. It is drawn from memory, notes, e-mail correspondence and business documents. It is a true story based on my best recollections of various events while working as an intelligence asset. Some of the details simply cannot be told.

The e-mail exchanges with intelligence agencies and documents confirming many of these operations are in my personal possession.

Some names and identifying characteristics of people and intelligence agents have been changed in order to protect their privacy. In some instances, the events and time periods have been compressed in order to serve the narrative. Dialogues are re-created to match my best recollections of these exchanges. No dramatic license was taken and no characters were invented or created from composites.

PROLOGUE

Not everyone understands the working life of a confidential informant (CI), but CI's play a crucial role in law enforcement and the shaping of world events. Informants pose as criminals so they can provide information to law enforcement or some government agency.

My recruitment as a CI happened in 2011 when I was approached by the CIA who were interested in the information I was handling as a result of my work in aviation and logistics.

Our world – the world of a CI - is a secret and largely unregulated world where there aren't any clear rules. Anything can happen. Quoting a former DEA informant, "You don't know whether you will get out of an operation alive … the fear is constant…."

To many people, the whole topic of confidential informants is a touchy subject. People simply aren't comfortable with the subject of informing. It evokes unease, discomfort wherever you are in the world. Indeed, there is a tradition against snitching in most societies.

Still, an informant is the most effective tool in intelligence operations today. Sure, there are satellites and other signal intelligence (SIGINT) methods readily available, but in order to know what the enemy is doing, what they are planning, or in order to verify information about their activities, requires human intelligence (HUMINT).

Human sources are vitally important to success against terrorists and criminals. They give critical intelligence and information that could not be obtained in other ways. Opening a window into an adversaries' plans and capabilities is crucial.

When my journey as an intelligence asset began, I was asked to continue with my work and not let on that I was communicating with the authorities. My orders were to pass on information as it became available.

Back then, and the same goes for now, I was haunted by the implications of following these orders. There were days when the whole topic of informing made me shudder. It was because I knew what I'd become and I knew people out there: shady underworld figures with no accountability and no conscience would see me and my family as snitches and therefore we were legitimate targets.

For some confidential informants, the motivation for informing is a cash reward, but for many others, including me, the risks taken and the work performed didn't have a price or a cash value. The transaction is much more simple than that. Whatever intelligence agency you are working for, you are expected to do what you are asked, whatever the cost. I became an informant as I believe in some kind of justice. In my eyes, I was doing something good. Something necessary. Something everyone could suffer for if I hesitated.

My reasons for acting as an informant have always been honorable. Since my first disclosure as an informant, I felt a duty to do what was right and to expose hypocrisy and corruption where I saw it. However, the consequences of this unique "employment" have never been straightforward.

Some consequences of my work have been life-changing. In the aftermath of exposing South African Deputy President

Kgalema Motlanthe (in office 2009-2014) and Gugu Mtshali, I've faced politically motivated "fraud" charges. After two assassination plots—one after I exposed a Pakistani heroin smuggling operation and another while in custody in July 2015, when my wife and child were targeted—and the stress of living amid a media frenzy, I've spent many years living without any sense of a "true freedom" that so many people take for granted.

My purpose for writing this book is not to bring credit to myself. Vanity is not at stake in this project. I would rather want this book to describe the operations CI's are normally involved with, to show what life as a confidential informant is like, the highs and lows, the drudgery and the excitement. Secrecy, of course, is the lifeblood of espionage. I am not a reckless renegade intent on exploiting clandestine operational details to promote a book.

I'd like to contribute something to the thin, necessarily sketchy patchwork of first-hand accounts we already have of what life is like for a confidential informant. The reader can judge for themselves the quality of the service of a CI in the cause of freedom. Willing to err on the side of openness, I chose the potential risks of telling my story. I trust in doing so will also serve the cause of freedom.

I also want to pay tribute to the unacknowledged work of informants and U.S. intelligence agents everywhere who have made excruciating sacrifices in the realization of that simple transaction every informant of an intelligence agency is faced with – the expectation that you will do what is asked of you, whatever the personal cost to you, with no going back and no medicine for the deep wounds that are often inflicted.

These people don't wear uniforms, and there are no shiny medals of honor for them to leave to grandchildren. There is no end to their workday, no time off and often, no going back. But in every hour that passes, they sacrifice what's precious and irreplaceable to them in the service of a yet to be realized greater good.

To catch wolves, you need wolves.

CHAPTER ONE

TEA IN TEHRAN

February 2007

T he cool, clean air of the Alborz mountains above Tehran provides escape and oxygen from the scramble of city life, and the endless movement of an upstart capital.

The Alborz are a place to relax, gaze down at the smog-shrouded city, catch the reflection of sunlight off glass, admire the snow-capped peaks above. The well-heeled entrepreneurs of Iran's capital like to kick back amid multi-course lunches in the restaurants that dot the hillsides, impress their guests and maybe clinch a deal or two.

But it's probably not too often that they entertain a 24-year old aviation enthusiast from South Africa.

And it was difficult for me to grasp – on that February afternoon in 2007 – that I was suddenly doing business in Iran – after a flurry of phone calls and email exchanges. A few miles away, the *bete noir* of the United States, President Mahmoud Ahmadinejad, was consolidating his power, a year into his first term in office. He seemed to relish the punishment of international sanctions that had followed Iran's decision in January 2006 to resume its nuclear research activities – ending a moratorium that had been agreed with the International Atomic Energy Agency.

A couple of thousand miles away, the Israelis were making noises – yet again - about taking out Iran's nuclear installations.

But my jovial host Hossein was oblivious to the international tension and the high stakes involved in busting sanctions. Perhaps he welcomed them as a source of high margins.

A golden haze hung above us, as if the sun was not in a single place but hammered thin and rolled across the sky like white-hot foil.

Unusually among the Iranians I met, Hossein was clean-shaven, with a mop of jet-black hair carefully parted at one side. His eyes were the darkest brown, verging on black, which made his expression hard to read at times. He was always well-dressed, but I could never work out whether he had five identical suits or just one that was lovingly pressed every night.

Hossein was an enterprising man. He wanted to find someone who knew the aircraft trade, who could find unwanted jumbo jets or helicopter rotors, and was not too worried about the fine print of UN resolutions and US Treasury directives.

Somehow he had found me – founder of 360 Aviation, a company that worked out of a dimly-lit hangar on the fringes of the prestigious Cape Town V & A Waterfront.

If we could help each other, he suggested, there would be plenty of money in it for both of us.

In 2007 Iran's reputation as a sponsor of terror, supporter of Hezbollah, schemer against US allies in the Middle East, destabilizer of Iraq, cloaked it in the image of international pariah.

How reputations mislead. In the few days I had been in Tehran I had felt welcomed, even feted. I had arrived at Imam

Khomeini Airport, which in itself sounded rather forbidding. But a friendly immigration official had asked me a few routine questions and wished me an enjoyable stay. My South African passport was welcome in the Islamic Republic of Iran as U.S passport had an inconvenient Israeli stamp on it, so it was safely tucked away at home.

A man with broken English and broken teeth held a name board in the chaotic arrivals area. He'd been sent by Hossein. His ready smile and insistence on taking my bag put me at ease.

As we walked into the bright sunshine, I struggled to take everything in: veiled women; austere, bearded men, the air permeated with the smell of cheap cigarettes.

And then there were the roads: Tehran's anarchic traffic as seen from my escort's battered Peugeot 206. Traffic signals appeared to be optional; turn indicators unnecessary. I was just glad I wasn't driving.

Most westerners would shudder at the prospect of visiting Tehran. Surely there were terrorists on every street corner, public executions, violent anti-western demonstrations. By far the greatest danger to any visitor is the way Tehrani's drive. It is no wonder that every vehicle has the scars of war. If they wanted to, the Iranians could field a world champion in rally-driving.

Tehran itself might be a city of modern anonymity, graceless and impatient. But I soon found that its people, one-on-one, were charming: they wanted to know about you and impress you. There was no hint of suspicion, nor a sense that they were glancing over your shoulder in case the secret police were watching the encounter from a discreet distance.

Hossein was a languorous character with a soft gaze and ready smile. His oft-expressed love of his family and the photographs of his children that were produced from his wallet at regular intervals gave him an avuncular presence. But he was also a survivor, a man who traded in contacts and favors, who remembered the days of the Shah and his sudden downfall. He knew better than most that pinning your flag to this party or that, one official or another, was not good business. You had to navigate the shoals.

Hossein was explaining all this over kebabs and *Tahdig* rice, and he had my attention. It was the essential preparation, my schooling, for the rollercoaster to come.

He seemed to know everyone and had arranged meetings with every company that had a plane in the air, or one on the ground that needed parts to fly again. Even the state carrier, Iran Air, wanted to meet me. But even as a budding entrepreneur with more enthusiasm than expertise I began to understand that their interest stemmed from the fact that I was one of a handful of foreigners ready to do business in Iran. And some of my potential clients were obscure 'trading companies' that had no passengers or scheduled services. Hossein, I would learn, was well connected even within the militant Iranian Revolutionary Guards Corps (IRGC), the chief exporter of the Islamic Republic's ideology and power.

In my defense, Iran didn't have the stain of leprosy among South Africans that it did in the United States. Relations were good; sanctions seemed overbearing to South African officials and were loosely interpreted.

Hossein was my guide and mentor through these encounters.

One evening – it must have gone 11pm – we sat down over yet another cup of tea and he gave me a history lesson.

The Islamic Republic had been starved of international technology almost since its birth in 1979. It was as if modernization had been frozen in aspic. Think Cuba, he said, conjuring images of 1950s Cadillacs and Buicks held together by wire and inelegant soldering.

"Well it's the same for us. In some ways, it's not a bad thing. We've become more self-reliant; we have to make things. But there's plenty we can't make. Like planes."

So Iran's airlines and freight carriers were quite literally flying on a wing and a prayer. Their planes were 30 years old and they had to scour the black market for replacement parts. To do so, they created front companies, elaborate trails of middlemen in parts of the world where government oversight was notoriously weak. Anything to throw Washington off the scent in the name of survival.

There was a sense of persecution among some of the executives I met. They were trying to fly people around in planes that would probably fail their airworthiness certificate in most countries. And across the Gulf, the wealthy Emirates flew a new fleet as a global carrier.

One of those executives was Dr Hossein Mansourian, an elegant man with a closely-shaved salt and pepper beard and a somewhat downcast demeanor, as might befit the head of procurement for Iran Air. He was already in touch with South African officials – who would soon invite him to visit, so he may have felt that I was in Tehran with the government's blessing. I wasn't – yet.

I was faintly amused but also somewhat over-awed by the fact that Iran's state carrier wanted to have lunch with the sole proprietor of a tiny South African company whose office would comfortably fit within my hotel room.

With almost an air of weariness, Mansourian explained the phenomenon of 'suicide companies' that Iran Air and other state entities used to evade sanctions. Companies would be set up as end-users in other countries only to evaporate the moment their purchases were loaded on freighters for Iran. And the purchases could range from a wing flap for an ageing 747 to a fuel pump for an equally venerable MD-80.

The Americans, he sighed, viewed such equipment as 'dual-use.' In other words, it could be used for military purposes as well as to repair a civilian plane.

The implication was that this was a ridiculous claim aimed at punishing Iran for daring to stand up to the 'Great Satan.' But Iran Air, I would later discover, wasn't solely interested in keeping its passenger timetable functioning. Like all state corporations in Iran, it served a higher purpose. Its planes – and those of carriers like Mahan and Saha – could be requisitioned by the likes of Iran's Revolutionary Guard Corps. The IRGC was (and is) one of the most militant parts of the Iranian establishment, combining its support of militia like Hezbollah in Lebanon with an ambitious weapons programme.[1]

Saha was actually a Farsi acronym for 'military transport service' and its ageing Airbus A300s were the workhorse of

---

1   On October 25th 2007, the United States designated the IRGC for its support to Iranian ballistic missile and nuclear programmes. Several IRGC entities and individuals are sanctioned under UN Security Council Resolutions 1737 and 1747.

the Iranian Air Force's resupply efforts to allies across the Middle East.

But in 2007 the complexities of the interlocking and often competing interests that made up the Islamic Republic were beyond me. Over ten days in Tehran I met a bewildering array of companies and government agencies, ignorant of the fact that beyond the shop window many had other functions.

One of our meetings was in a quiet side-street, a rarity itself in the Iranian capital. The venue was the modest office of Heli-Kish, whose two rooms had a few scruffy chairs and chipped wooden desks. I suddenly felt better about the headquarters of 360 Aviation.

A male receptionist whose desk did not suggest he was overwhelmed with work greeted us and escorted us to the inner office, where Alireza Valadkhani, owner of Heli-Kish, awaited.

Valadkhani – a slight man who could have been taken for an academic - was immaculately dressed in a way very much at odds with his surroundings. He had greying hair and a habit of pursing his lips whenever he finished speaking. He also had a lazy eye, and I struggled not to get drawn to it as we talked.

Valadkhani was nothing if not confident in his own abilities. He knew how to import a helicopter into Iran – bypassing sanctions as if swatting a fly. But he was always looking for new opportunities.

"There are some Bell 212s in Israel that are surplus to requirements," I told him. "Not a bad price, but they'd have to come via somewhere in Europe to disguise the buyer."

"One careful owner: the Israeli Defense Forces," I added,

trying to make a joke of their origin. It didn't go down well.

The Bell 212 was a medium-sized helicopter that was a classic 'dual-role' aircraft, in both civilian and military roles. Transport, fire-fighting, even anti-submarine warfare: there were many variants.

Valadkhani remained impassive, apparently unimpressed and uncommitted.

"Don't worry," Hossein said as we left Heli-Kish. "It's the way he does business; never says much and then makes a decision."

And so the encounters went on – could I procure this or source that? At the back of my mind, I appreciated that much of the Iranian shopping list would be viewed with suspicion in Washington. But I took comfort from the very deliberate courting of Iran by my own government back in Pretoria – partly because of the deals that might come about but also to strike a pose independent of the West.

On my last evening in Tehran, I sat exhausted in my hotel, transfixed by the skyline. Shades of pearl and mustard intertwined as twilight approached. The setting sun illuminated the mountains in shades of pink and purple. I liked the place, felt an affinity for its people. Getting the Iranians planes that wouldn't crash because of old age seemed entirely legitimate; but the rubric of international sanctions suggested otherwise.

Beyond that vague self-justification for what I was doing, I was simply enjoying myself too much – meeting important people who wanted my help, deal-making, jetting from exotic destination to the next. It was so dazzling that I was blinded to the less palatable consequences that might lie down the road.

Arguments about the free market and the black market – they could wait. I could not guess that I was about to embark on a long, tortuous and sometimes dark journey that would lead me into trading everything from helicopters to guns to cigarettes and heroin.

CHAPTER TWO

HURRICANE BARRY
September 1983

Perhaps my restless nature was prescribed by the circumstances of my birth, on September 1st 1983. Hurricane Barry had just made landfall in southern Texas. Amid deserted streets and floods and wreckage tossed in every direction, my mother Elza went into labor in a Houston maternity ward.

She was a calm, almost placid woman, for whom giving birth held no terrors. She delivered four children with little fuss, of whom I was the third.

Mum was also the foundation stone of our family, a woman of steadfast resilience. Maybe I was more a product of that hurricane, hurled onto this earth with great ferocity. Appropriately, a life of tempestuous upheaval lay in wait, one that would toss me like debris from one crisis to the next.

But I could take the metaphor too far. I wasn't named after the hurricane but after my father, Barend. The family was in Houston because he was serving at the South African consulate-general in the city – a diplomat in the fast lane.

Dad was an intelligent, perceptive man, but he was more than that. He was wise. He immersed himself in the affairs of the world; and was typically buried in a newspaper, a cigarette dangling between his fingers. One of eight children, his father had fought in the Second World War. He had entered the diplomatic service after making his name as a criminal defense attorney, his agile mind perhaps better suited to the cut and thrust of the courtroom rather than protocols of state. And he might have made a successful politician – he'd become mayor of the town of Vredenburg on South Africa's Atlantic coast at the age of just 26.

My father travelled a great deal, so it was my mother who tried to provide us – my brother, two sisters and I - with structure and self-discipline. She was also immensely sympathetic, sensitive to our troubles, striking an immaculate balance between protecting us and straightening our backs. And at the same time she combined family duty with a successful career selling real estate. She was the quintessential multi-tasker, unflappable and supremely organized.

I have just fragments of memories about our return to South Africa. I wasn't even four. But I can recall the tea boxes littering our suburban Houston home; and climbing up the steps for my first plane ride.

I was 'returning' to my homeland, though I had no idea what that meant. Surely, we were leaving home, not returning anywhere.

In the late 1980s, South Africa was on the verge of historic change. The apartheid regime was being dismantled by the political class that had benefited so much from it, much like Mikhail Gorbachev was uprooting a system that had benefited the communist party elite in the Soviet Union. Except that in South Africa there was real apprehension among the white minority that had ruled for so long that majority rule would bring with it a thirst for revenge.

Unbeknown to me, Dad was one of the backroom negotiators with the African National Congress as the end of apartheid was being negotiated. There was a framed photograph in his study of himself, former President P.W. Botha and ANC negotiator Tokyo Sexwale together. As a kid of eight or nine I noticed it, but only understood its significance years later. I am proud to possess it to this day.

These were heady times, but such profound and rapid change brings with it chronic uncertainty – and that uncertainty seeps into a boy not yet in his teens.

We lived a comfortable life in the northern suburbs of Cape Town. My father was Director of the Bureau of Information, a well-paid and prominent position. My older brother, Marcel, had a much better idea of the profound transformation taking place. He was already well into his teens and closer to my father. They were similar: reserved, quiet to the point of shy, slow to make friends and content with their own company. Marcel would follow in Dad's footsteps – he would study law and they'd go into business many years later after my Dad left government service.

I was the third of four children - two boys and two girls. The girls inherited a combination of my mother's common sense and diligence, and my father's intellect. My older sister Lizanne would become a medical trauma surgeon in Canada after what seemed like endless courses and exams. My younger sister Zithe, mastered German and became a lawyer in New York after being a valedictorian in her post graduate scholarships. They were straight A students who won scholarships wherever they went, and both ultimately decided that life beyond South Africa held greater opportunities and professional challenges.

I inherited my father's enthusiasm for rugby, very much the white man's preserve even in the 1990s. I turned out to be pretty good at it – fast and strong and unflinching in the tackle. At the age of 13 I was made captain of the Western Province junior team. And it was my athletic ability that won me a place at one of South Africa's most prestigious boarding schools: Paul Roos Gymnasium, in the historic town of Stellenbosch.

Entering PRG, as it was ubiquitously known, was like walking through the history of white South Africa. It had been the proving ground of Prime Ministers and, as importantly, many rugby players who had gone on to play for the fabled Springboks, the national team long excluded from international competition because of apartheid. In fact, PRG had spawned more Springboks than any other school in South Africa, an achievement of which we were frequently reminded.

It was a strange feeling, being part of South Africa's defiant and proud history just as the country was about to change out of recognition. But it wasn't something I spent much time thinking about. Teenage boys on the whole don't have much time for the past. Life was all about sport, girls (a perennial fantasy in an all-male boarding school) and making solid friendships, with academic demands trailing in the distance. Classes were to be endured rather than enjoyed, although PRG had a good academic record and was about much more than a tracksuit ethic.

I was one of the more rebellious boys, and surrounded myself with similar spirits. The greatest challenge of boarding school was escaping it, through gates and over walls, and preferably at night. The lure of the girls' boarding school just along the Eerste River was a temptation worthy of a Greek odyssey.

I was barely sixteen when a group of us absconded on a crisp autumn evening with the wholly laudable aim of serenading the girls in their dormitories. My friend Christopher – with whom I played rugby for Western Province – thought we should treat the girls to our full glory as we sang. And he stripped off as we arrived outside their quarters.

Such a challenge could not go unanswered, and within minutes a posse of naked teenagers were sprinting past the dorm windows, whistling for attention. Not surprisingly, we got it. The girls crowded around the windows and I swear some were cheering.

Unfortunately, they were not the only ones to notice the commotion. The school's patrol vehicle swept around the corner in hot pursuit of the visitors, and we scattered – panicking that the vehicle would reach us before we reached our clothes. Poor Chris had the bright idea of going over the roof – only to lose his balance and end up perched on a windowsill in full view of an ongoing Parent Teachers' meeting. I still laugh out loud with the recollection of that escapade.

Boarding school can be tough: self-reliance and a thick skin are necessities. But it also provides structure, predictability – notable by their absence when I finally stepped beyond the walls of PRG for the final time in the summer of 2001.

I did take rugby with me, choosing to represent the country of my birth rather than that of my heritage. And just months out of PRG I found myself in Italy, representing the United States' Under-19 Eagles at an international tournament. In between games, we were taken on a variety of excursions, and one of them was to the home of the US Air Force 31st Fighter Wing at Aviano.

As I stood inside a hangar of F-16 combat jets, every other aspect of my life melted into insignificance. I was overawed by the display of speed, power and engineering brilliance, by the sleek shape of these supersonic predators. The image remains with me: those few minutes in a hushed hangar changed my life.

As we left the base, the Commanding Officer presented us with medals. "Perhaps some of you will even think of joining the United States Air Force and serving your country, just as you are playing for your country now," he said.

I couldn't imagine a career in the military – not after just shedding the restrictions of boarding school. But I knew I wanted to fly. And back in South Africa I soon found the man who would help me.

His name was Neil – a wiry, humorous character in his thirties who was site manager for a company called Starlite Aviation. The company had a base adjacent to Cape Town airport and specialized in training helicopter pilots.

Neil sported a buzz cut that always had me wondering whether his hair was brown or ginger. He never let it grow out so the question was never answered. He always wore a pair of Rayban aviators and could have been taken for a Special Forces officer.

Well-educated, precise and persuasive in speech, Neil was

one of the best helicopter pilots I have ever known. He also had a flair for figures and a salesman's patter. To me, at the age of 21, he seemed the renaissance man. He was one of those rare characters you warm to within minutes of your first meeting. His passion for flying immediately deepened mine; he recognized in me one of the brotherhood for whom being in the sky was an addiction that couldn't be kicked.

Flying was also a form of escape, as I also realized at the time. My parents' marriage – which had seemed to me as solid as Table Mountain – had unraveled. My father had always liked a drink; now he seemed to need more than one as he brooded alone in an apartment.

My promising rugby career had brought the best out of him. He would clear all obstacles to attend my games. But a niggling knee injury had kept me off the playing field for months; he no longer had the incentive to emerge from his self-imposed shell.

I was living with my mother, who seemed both sad and even a little embarrassed by what had happened. But as always, she coped. Ultimately, she was stronger than Dad – even if he was the intellectual powerhouse. But she worried about me, and the effect their separation had on all four children.

Her anxiety grew when I unceremoniously dumped my marketing degree course at the University of South Africa in 2004. I was 21; my eyes were on the sky.

CHAPTER THREE

HIGH FLYER
2004

Neil soon moved from Starlite Aviation to another company, Base 4. And I followed him. They had no job openings, but my naïve determination amused and faintly impressed them. I was setting out in an industry dominated by well-funded corporate players, in which I had no qualifications. But there is always a niche – and I loved living on my wits, pitching ideas and harnessing contacts.

My first venture was simple enough: helicopter rides for the well-heeled arranged through a contact in the tourist industry. Base 4 were quickly onboard, recognizing a fresh stream of revenue for their fleet of choppers. I would organize flights to festivals and game parks, and would split the profit with the company.

By now my father and brother Marcel had started a business together – and were making respectable profits with a handful of small vermiculite and granite mines. They probably hoped that I would join them. But if they did, they hid their disappointment when I struck out on my own. They even provided financial support for the grandly named Peninsula Executive, which I created just weeks after quitting college.

I had only just started: I wanted to do the flying myself.

My instructor was Frank, a veteran pilot in his sixties, lanky and silver-haired. He was businesslike and focused; we were after all flying an expensive piece of machinery. And he knew how to coax the best out of both his pupil and the chopper.

"The aerodynamic principles are the same as on an airplane," Frank explained as we were going through the basic principles of flight.

I knew how a helicopter stayed in the air and I had been out for a few rides with friends who were pilots, but I had to start with the basics. Frank was a demanding instructor.

"Those blades serve the same function as the wing on an airplane," he said as we walked around a little Robinson 22 helicopter on the apron.

"The only difference is that a wing is attached to the fuselage, whereas these turn. And that creates lift."

I glanced up at the rotor blades; the distinctive whiff of jet fuel was hanging in the air.

"See that little rotor at the end of the tail boom?" He pointed toward the rear of the helicopter. "It does all the things for stability and directional control on the helicopter that your tail does on an airplane, and then some."

It was time to put theory into action. I will never forget the words of Air Traffic Control.

"Romeo Tango Foxtrot, you are cleared for take-off."

Frank deftly lifted the machine off the ground and we hovered for a few moments before he pushed the stick forward. The Robinson dipped, its skids almost touching the concrete.

It was an April morning of glittering clarity in 2004; the cloudless sky was a rain-washed deep blue, the air crisp.

"You have control," Frank's voice crackled over the

headphones. My hands and feet were stiff against the controls, making the helicopter weave off balance.

Rather than admonish me, Frank's matter-of-fact delivery made me feel at ease.

"Try to relax, small movements."

I never wanted the flight to end. The world beneath looked remote, manageable, shorn of its problems and challenges. To the west, the Atlantic waves were tiny streaks of white breaking on Robben Island, where Nelson Mandela – former President – had spent so long in prison. To the south, Table Mountain in all its glory – one of the seven natural wonders of the world - stood sentry over the ocean and the Cape Town Centre.

As dots moved along roads and the endless horizon stretched into the ocean, an indefinable sense of serenity came over me. Serenity and a sense of superiority – as the master of the elements, answerable to no-one, looking down on the earth and its petty squabbles.

But learning to fly doesn't come cheap. I needed a job, and wasn't beyond begging Base 4's Chief Executive, Darryl Waterford. Darryl came from a wealthy family, and some in the industry carped that Base 4 only survived because of his father's money. But Darryl was a canny, resilient operator and was building Base 4 into one of the biggest helicopter operators in Africa.

To begin with, the company wasn't wild about hiring a greenhorn, despite my evidently incurable addiction to flight.

In the end my nagging wore him down. As I prepared for another lesson with all the buoyancy of a puppy spaniel, Darryl called me into his office.

"So," he said," leaning back in his high-backed leather chair with the trace of a grin on his face, "I hear you are looking for a job."

He was enjoying being the puppet-master; he knew I was dangling.

"We want to start a sales division and I am willing to give you a trial period of three months. The basic salary will be small but we can share the commission. If you don't sell anything in 3 months, we call it quits."

I could scarcely contain myself. I leapt up and extended my hand.

"Thanks Darryl, I won't disappoint you."

Like a demented plane-spotter, I wrote down all the tail numbers of the fleet of helicopters in the hangar, and then hit the phones to prospective buyers and sellers. I had to understand the mentality and the hard-headed business motives of my customers, for whom buying and selling helicopters was an investment. There was also maintenance work to be pitched for, so the company could also make money after the sale.

I loved the challenge of selling and had the persistence it demanded, learning quickly the art of navigating the network of gatekeepers that tried to keep you from the man with the money. Personal assistants, secretaries and assorted hangers-on had to be sweet-talked to gain entry to the inner sanctum - and the cheque book.

I was driven on by the fact that I had walked out on my undergraduate course. I had a point to prove: that success didn't require letters after your name

I sold nine helicopters in a seven-month period which

included six ex-military SA 316 Alouettes. At the age of 22, I was grossing $10,000 a month. In one spectacular month I made off with $30,000 in commissions. I even arranged all of Sir Richard Branson's helicopter transfers while he was launching Virgin Mobile in South Africa.

But there were even richer pickings beyond South Africa.

CHAPTER FOUR

FOR WHOM THE BELLS TOLL
2006

Base 4 liked to 'punch above their weight', as the saying has it. It was a small, feisty firm. But Darryl and Neil, now its sales director, had bigger ambitions.

Neil and I both had deal-making in our bloodstreams. The money smelt good of course, but it was just as much about the sport – the pitching, the persuasion, the coaxing and the compromises to clinch that critical signature. We bonded: the young, outgoing buccaneer and the sales professional, scouring the small print, deciding the tactics.

All over the world, as military forces modernize, their old equipment becomes surplus to requirements. There is a second-hand market in everything from tanks to howitzers to helicopters. Some of the equipment is in poor shape, not worth looking at. But the Israeli Defense Forces are always modernizing, wanting the best. And when they get it, they maintain it. So when we found out that the Israeli Air Force had a handful of Bell-212 helicopters on offer, we were soon on our way.

For me, the excitement of foreign terrain was enough in itself. We landed in Tel Aviv late in the evening on a mild April evening in 2006. The air was humid as we stepped out of the airport terminal at Ben Gurion – a faint whiff of sea air mixing with airport fumes.

I was used to seeing plenty of police on the streets; South Africa was renowned for its urban violence. But by the time we had arrived at our sea-front hotel in Tel Aviv, I had begun to appreciate that Israel was different – a country perpetually on a war footing. I was struck by the contrast: wealthy foreigners and Israelis enjoying watermelon martinis and jazz in a plush hotel bar while well-armed soldiers patrolled outside.

Our hosts were veteran Israeli arms dealers, Shaked Agmon and Serge Muller.

Muller made his name in the diamond business in Belgium, joining his family company S. Muller and Sons Diamonds NV, a famous Antwerp-based firm, decades ago.

For years, he dealt in diamonds across the world - from Canada to South Africa – building up considerable wealth and an international network of companies.

His best known company, Rex Mining, was incorporated in 1990 in Canada, with a license to trade in diamonds in Belgium and shares in a mine in South Africa and Sierra Leone, a country infamous for so-called 'blood diamonds' - illegally mined gems traded for weapons destined for use in brutal civil wars.

Muller was also involved in supplying weapons to Sierra Leone. In 1998, he sold engines, parts and ammunition for the state's only combat helicopter, which the government used to fight the Revolutionary United Front (RUF), Sierra Leone's rebel army, in an eleven-year war from 1991 to 2002.

Shaked shrugged as he amiably explained the context to someone for whom history classes had never held much appeal.

"For 1500 years Christians, Jews and Muslims have struggled

over the Holy Land. The struggle goes on. We founded our homeland fifty years ago, but the Palestinians still can't accept it."

And at that point Israel was enduring a campaign of suicide bombings. Militant groups, such as Islamic Jihad, were intent on terror attacks against Israeli civilians.

Neil and I spent several days inspecting the Bells at different sites. They had been demilitarized – all the sensitive and lethal equipment stripped out – but we reluctantly concluded that too much work was required to adapt them for the US client we had in mind.

We were both disappointed; this was to be our first foray into the big-time and the cost of the trip was hardly negligible. We left the Bells behind, but they would return to haunt me.

'Interested parties' were sitting in Tehran, the same city where support for Islamic Jihad and other militant Islamist groups was planned, the same city where President Mahmoud Ahmadinejad was railing against Israel's very existence.

Despite the disappointment of not clinching a deal, Neil clearly saw potential in our partnership. Soon after we arrived home, we went for a drink after work.

"So I have a proposal," he said after downing his beer in about three gulps.

"You, me, your brother," he said. "Our own venture. You have the gift of persuasion, you're presentable, 'clubbable' as they say. And your brother is smart; he has commercial experience. And I have the industry experience. I just don't want to be doing the same thing for Base 4 in ten years from now."

I had introduced Neil to my brother a few months earlier. They had immediately got on. Neil saw his quiet, methodical approach as a good counterpoint to my preference for seeing life as a game of roulette, where putting everything on black seemed as good a strategy as any.

Within weeks we had created our own venture, while doing our best to stay on good terms with the crew at Base 4. Exec Heli was born in December 2006; Peninsula Executive was laid to rest with some sadness.

CHAPTER FIVE

LOVE, CHOPPERS & CLUBBING
2006-07

Back in Cape Town I went into sales overdrive, building a rolodex of contacts, developing an online site to advertise the helicopters we had and other services we could offer. Pride was at stake – my bold decision to strike out on my own was beginning to look foolhardy. And besides my family, I had someone else to impress.

Ever the entrepreneur, I had begun to explore the possibility of a business venture with a night-club owner. It wasn't really my scene, but he was someone I knew and trusted – and I was beginning to have doubts that the helicopter venture would ever pay my bills.

The club was high-end and immensely popular with the 'young affluents' of Cape Town, which as a city also happened to be home to an unreasonably large number of beautiful women. I walked in one night to find it crowded with an almost indecent number of them.

There could have been a thousand; it would have made no difference. My attention was fixed on just one – a slim, blonde woman about my age with a presence that defied description.

Unable to take my eyes off her, and studying her every movement and gesture, I stumbled toward the bar. The man she seemed to be with was also standing there.

"Veuve Cliquot, two glasses," he said with the confidence of a man for whom such an order was routine and hang the expense. I felt as if he'd hit me in the solar plexus rather than ordered a bottle of champagne.

As he waited, I took a leap into the unknown. Maybe he would hit me after all.

"Is that your girlfriend?" I asked, nodding to the blonde, a study in poise and beauty.

I was ready with a conciliatory follow-up line about his good fortune. But rather than tell me to mind my own business, he smiled.

"No, no – we are just friends."

I could tell he wished it were otherwise, and could only pray he didn't seal the deal that evening.

I had to wait for my moment and it came when Champagne Boy recognized a group of friends entering the club. Left alone for a few minutes, she began to study her cell-phone, the time-honored retreat of anyone suddenly left to their own devices for a few minutes.

"Now or never," I muttered to myself.

My introduction was hardly fluent or casual; I was unable to disguise my helpless infatuation. But she smiled and her gentle, sympathetic eyes only deepened that infatuation a few notches.

I knew I didn't have long so after a few minutes of agonizing small talk, I lied when I told her that her workplace was close to mine (I didn't think it the right moment to tell her that I spent much of my working life in a draughty airport hangar) and suggested lunch one day.

"Sure," she said, smiling. "That would be fun."

Her name was Munique and I was in love; there was no other way to put it. I had had plenty of girlfriends; but the relationships rarely extended from weeks to months. None had made such a deep, immediate, almost disturbing impact on first sight.

So just as I needed to concentrate at work, I had a serious distraction to contend with. I was ridiculously nervous before our lunch meeting, agonizing over the perfect venue – not too formal but not too basic. I changed shirts several times and spent twice what I normally would on a haircut.

I felt like a schoolboy again, pacing back and forth in the hours before our first 'date' – unable to concentrate on anything. I hardly noticed an email from an unlikely place and a man I had never heard of: Hossein, the Tehran-based wheeler-dealer and a very different lunch partner.

Sometimes, the need – almost the desperation – to make some money or kick-start a business blinds you to the consequences. You start to justify to yourself the shadier side of a deal, take short cuts that would not go down well at business school. And in the middle of 2007, trying to impress the woman of my dreams and keep my alliance with Neil alive, need was fast becoming desperation.

And so it was that I left Cape Town on that odyssey to Tehran, where I arrived dizzy after four flights and several time zones. The encounters on that trip, which begin this book, were to change my life. When I returned home, it was straight into Munique's arms. She came to meet me at the airport, with a smile that would light up the Empire State building. We were a couple and I knew the definition of euphoria. It would be just months before we were engaged; and just a few more before we married.

*

I had promised Hossein I would work my contacts in the South African government to begin getting the approvals needed to do business in Iran. I was talking a good game; my contacts scarcely extended beyond an annual encounter with the tax man.

But I was nothing if not resourceful, and my previous experience selling planes to men with money would come in helpful. Neil, Marcel and I made our way steadily up the ladder of officialdom until we landed a meeting with the Deputy Director General of the Department of Trade . His name was Iqbal Sharma, and he would later be caught up in a scandal over a tendering process in which he had what might euphemistically be called a conflict of interest.[2]

I was almost as nervous as I had been before my lunch with Munique. Sharma had absolute power over the department's export permissions. He was also the point man for South Africa's burgeoning commercial relationship with Iran.

The South African government, led by President Thabo Mbeki, was travelling in the opposite direction to the US in its relationship with Iran. As the US tightened sanctions, and pressured its closest allies to follow suit, Pretoria saw opportunities in filling the void. The previous year, Sharma had taken part in extensive discussions with a visiting delegation

---

2   http://mg.co.za/article/2014-07-03-transnet-tender-bosss-r50-billion-double-game

led by Iran's Foreign Minister, Manouchehr Mottaki.[3]
The visit had led to all sorts of promises about promoting trade; Iran was hungry for any technology it could lay its hands on – from agriculture to railways. South Africa badly wanted to sell to Iran to mitigate a large deficit caused by oil imports.[4]

Sharma was already in touch with some of the people I had met in Tehran, and would a short time later write a letter to Iran Air's head of planning, Hossein Mansourian, noting "the backdrop of our strong political relationship and growing economic relationship."[5]

We were, thankfully, pushing at a door that was already half-open.

After we had taken pains to emphasize that our proposal was solely to do with maintaining commercial aircraft, he agreed to issue a letter of support. It was the breakthrough we needed, and just in time; Hossein was beginning to doubt our good faith.

We invited a number of Iranian clients to Cape Town, among them the boss of Heli-Kish, the saturnine Alireza Valadkhani. He had found a helicopter in Canada, but needed to ship it via a third country with a more liberal interpretation of sanctions. There weren't many left: Europe and even the Gulf countries, under US pressure, were tightening up.

But of course there were ways to circumvent sanctions: elaborate routes, descriptions of exports that were artful and

3   http://www.dirco.gov.za/docs/2006/iran0823a.htm
4   In 2010, South Africa imported about 40% of its oil from Iran.
5   In 2008 the Department of Trade issued two letters of support to 360 Aviation signed by Sharma: on 5 February and 3 September.

inventive, a mesh of companies that were here today and gone tomorrow. Even the US Treasury and the CIA couldn't keep track of every transaction. And I continued to tell myself that what we were doing was fair. There were no weapons involved, nor technology that would make them. But I was deceiving myself. I knew the Iranians were trying to reverse engineer the technology they were able to obtain.

Valadkhani's plan was certainly elaborate. A Canadian company called Eagle Copters had bought a 1979 Bell 212 helicopter from Hudson Flight in Texas. It would sell the chopper to a South African front company called Gemini Moon Trading 477, registered in Johannesburg. Gemini Moon was wholly owned by a trust, whose beneficiaries were two of Valadkhani's associates, Malek Sabet and Houshang Shans

Valadkhani arrived in Cape Town in January 2009. He looked just slightly less confident in such unfamiliar surroundings, perhaps unbalanced by the sight of so many long-legged South African beauties walking the streets in mini-skirts.

We settled around the rather grand mahogany desk that belied Exec Heli's status as a fledgling outfit hungry for business – any business.

"So Mr Valadkhani, what is it then that you would like us to do?"

Valadkhani scratched his beard for a few moments. He'd become no more animated since we'd met in Tehran.

"I just want you to oversee the logistics. We will arrange everything else. You get the aircraft registered here and then do the de-registration paperwork."

Valadkhani was a tough negotiator. He liked bargaining and

enjoyed poring over the details. But he was not just negotiating with us; he had to deal with layers of Iranian bureaucracy. He had the patience and persistence of a dog sure that he had buried a bone somewhere.

Once he was persuaded that the helicopter he was buying would get to and out of South Africa, Valadkhani left for home. We were pleased with ourselves: the deal wasn't huge but we had mastered its complexities and fully expected follow-on business.

But progress was painfully slow. A second Iranian delegation turned out to be more interested in South Africa's wineries and strip clubs than might be expected of devout Muslims. There was sporadic contact from Valadkhani. We relied on helicopter tourism to make ends meet, but that was seasonal. Cape Town could be wet and battered by gales in the southern winter.

My wedding to Munique was coming up; and I wanted somewhere to live where she would be safe and comfortable. I needed cash – and the Vacca Matta nightclub seemed the surest (and most tempting) way to make it.

Vacca Matta was on the 'Strip' in Edward Street – Cape Town's Northern suburbs entertainment district during that time. It had an up-market clientele, sports stars, models and celebrities. The overheads were considerable but so was the potential. And owning a nightclub seemed the epitome of glamour. You walked straight past the velvet rope of hopeful customers, famous names would greet you, the champagne would flow.

The image was enticing enough; the reality wildly different. Neil, my brother and I decided to invest in Vacca Matta, and within months were not so much struggling to stay afloat as deeply submerged.

Running any business requires financial discipline, attention to detail, hiring the right people. Running a nightclub requires all that in spades - as well as nurturing a solid brand in a fickle market. Employees who handed out free drinks to clients, belligerent customers, local authorities with the power to grant and revoke permits and licenses – all conspired against us. The competition was fierce, the trade dead four nights a week. No wonder the people selling Vacca Matta looked so relieved when the deal was concluded. We should have noticed.

Six months later we were the sellers, offloading the place for half of what we had paid – not counting the improvements we had made to the club. The experience put a great deal of strain on my relationship with my brother; it's easy to start playing the blame game when things start going south. Nor did it help my new marriage; hemorrhaging cash was not the best way to start out.

It was almost a relief to learn that Mr Valadkhani was coming back. He might be taciturn and difficult, but at least I had some rudimentary knowledge of the airplane business. And his Bell 212 was finally arriving from Canada.

It was a bitterly cold night in June 2009. I stood in the cargo area of Oliver Tambo International airport in Johannesburg as the KLM Boeing 747 freighter taxied to a standstill, shooting clouds of dust across the tarmac.

The news from KLM was not good. A pallet had shifted during turbulence and hit the horizontal stabilizer of the helicopter. An omen perhaps, but there was nothing to do but get it fixed. Insurance would pay for the damage but we still had to get the machine to the nearest Bell maintenance facility 50 kilometres away.

Valadkhani wasn't happy to hear the news; and we had to offer repeated assurances that all would be fine – especially when the week of repairs turned into a month. But eventually, I got a call from the Bell distributor. helicopter – with its ZS-HDF South African registration – was ready for collection.

'HDF' was rapidly becoming the most cossetted helicopter in the world. Now it had to be prepared for another journey, aboard a giant Ilyushin 76 cargo jet – destination Kish Island, Iran. The price – a one-way ticket - was a mere $275,000.

The Ilyushin was the freighter of choice for all sorts of anonymous carriers, whose planes carried few markings and obscure registrations. Its slanting wings gave it a somewhat forlorn appearance, but it was the rugged cart-horse of cargo jets. And it had a secret. Beneath the floor of its hold was space for a further 13 tonnes of cargo, in large chambers. The chambers were unknown to many customs authorities, and loading them could severely test the plane's capacity – but for some companies and pilots it was a risk worth taking.

It helped that the Il-76 was able to take plenty of punishment. It had been designed for basic airstrips and in typically Soviet style built for survival rather than performance. I was really looking forward to seeing one up close. But I'd have to wait longer than expected. Storms over east Africa delayed the Ukrainian-registered plane by several hours. It was almost dawn when it arrived and began offloading – at a hectic pace – its seemingly never-ending cargo.

At last, I thought, as the Bell was loaded, an assignment finally completed. I left Johannesburg airport quietly satisfied and determined to reinvigorate my efforts after the Vacca Matta disaster.

The call followed a couple of hours later.

"The aircraft had to turn around due to an engine light that came on," the charter broker said. "It's about to arrive back in Johannesburg"

"How long do we anticipate the downtime?" I asked, burying my head in my hands.

"We can't say until the crew can take a look. We will be in touch once we have news."

Two weeks later, the engine was repaired, the plane flew and Mr Valadkhani was the proud owner of one well-travelled US-made Bell 212 helicopter.

I was in the sanctions-busting business, and really quite enjoying it.

When the deal became public, reported in South Africa's *Sunday Times* years later, the Department of Trade professed to being shocked that I had dispatched a Bell 212 to Iran.

"360 Aviation [said they were only selling] helicopters for civilian use," the Department told the *Sunday Times.*

"A letter of support will never be issued by the DTI in contravention of specific international agreements. The DTI does not engage in sanctions-busting," it continued disingenuously.

It's all in the eye of the beholder, I thought.

Valadkhani was also trying to get his hands on some of those former Israeli Bells, through a deal with a couple of

Spanish businessmen. I would later become intimately familiar with the saga, much to Valadkhani's distress.

But at the end of 2007, I had another deal to clinch. I rented a six-bedroom mansion on the slopes of the Hottentot-Holland mountains for a weekend and invited family and some close friends to join Munique and myself for a relaxing weekend. The mountains rose majestically above Gordon's Bay, south east of Cape Town, and their slopes offered magnificent views to the vineyards below and the ocean beyond. To be honest, I couldn't really afford such an extravagance, but it was an important investment.

Munique and I arrived on the Friday afternoon, and I went to work – preparing by my standards a very appetizing dinner and cooling the best white wine South Africa had to offer. The table was candle-lit, the tranquillity utterly soothing, the air cooled by a breeze. In the distance, the lights of Stellenbosch twinkled.

The piece de resistance was my home-made crème brulee, which was firm enough to hold an engagement ring. So low was the light that Munique did not see it at first and I had a frisson of terror that she would swallow it. But at the last second she spotted it.

"What's this?" she asked. But she knew instantly. By the time she looked at me I was already sinking to one knee – and asking for her hand in marriage.

The wedding that followed a few months later was a lavish affair at a five-star golf resort near Hermanus. We took over the whole hotel, with some 100 guests, and the dancing continued until the sun rose

CHAPTER SIX

THE SUICIDE COMPANY
2008-09

I wasn't the only one attracted to the lucrative if risky Iranian market for aircraft and choppers. And I wasn't the only one to perceive that South Africa, with its lax regulation, was a useful entrepot for such ventures.

As I was finalizing the Valadkhani deal, I received a call from a Dutch businessman, Rutger Koolhaas. His first enquiry, about some planes we were selling as brokers, was innocent enough.

But then he began asking for advice on how to set up a local company and whether it could be used to register aircraft imported from abroad. It wasn't long before I discovered a new company in the aviation business. Tigris International was registered in Groblersdal, a farming town north-east of Johannesburg with no airport and one street. Its directors were Koolhaas and his local partner Herman Venter. The main shareholder was an Iranian: Bijan Pakdaman.

In 2009 Tigris clinched a deal worth almost two billion rand (at that time about $200 million) to buy six Airbus A-300s from China Southern Airlines. But they knew that China Southern – as an international carrier – would not want to get embroiled in any form of sanctions busting. So Koolhaas and Pakdaman set up an elaborate web of front companies to show the aircraft would be owned by South African entities. They also secured funding guarantees issued by a Danish bank, ostensibly to an Iranian cosmetics concern.

Koolhaas was using a device known as 'suicide companies' to evade sanctions. He would register aircraft with a shelf company with no assets, which he would buy for probably $50. Once the aircraft were exported to Iran, he would wind up the company. To buy the Airbuses he created Streamland Air, and in August 2009 they touched down at Lanseria airport – a privately-held operation – north of Johannesburg.

The cosmetics company in Kish Island was called – unsurprisingly - Kish Cosmetics. It was part of the Sorinet Group owned by Iranian billionaire Babak Zanjani.

Zanjani would later be blacklisted by the US and European Union on the grounds of "assisting designated entities to violate the provisions of the sanctions against Iran," and was identified as "a key facilitator for Iranian oil deals and transferring oil-related money."

He later admitted to creating an array of companies - based in the United Arab Emirates, Turkey and Malaysia - to sell millions of barrels of Iranian oil on behalf of the government, generating $17.5bn of desperately needed revenue.[6]

In the end, because of a dispute over terms, only one of the Chinese Airbuses left South Africa for Iran, arriving on Kish Island on December 18th 2009. Less than two years later the plane was transferred to Meraj Airlines. And Meraj Airlines

6   Zanjani would later be charged with fraud and embezzlement by the Iranian authorities. He was convicted and sentenced to death. The government claimed he had stolen $1.9 billion in oil revenues.

used the plane to ferry cargo, personnel and weapons from Tehran to Syria.

Some of the weapons landed up in Lebanon with Hezbollah, designated as a terror group by the US and other countries.[7] Without the South African connection, that Airbus might never have made it to Iran. But it did, and it became the shuttle between Tehran and Damascus that helped keep the Assad regime afloat.[8]

I had many phone calls with Koolhaas, offering guidance on the South African market and regulations. Every time we talked it seemed that he was about to offer me a percentage of the deal for my help. He hinted at it and thanked me frequently. But later I realized that he never had any intention to bring me on board; he was just milking me for as much information as possible. It was another lesson.

Not every effort to evade international sanctions succeeded. It was like a game of hide and seek, except played out on a global stage with expensive machinery and frequently ruthless players, like Koolhaas and Zanjani.

Sometimes governments too could move with surprising speed and take an uncompromising line - even when there was

---

7   "Meraj Air is a Government of Iran airline that has been used to ferry illicit cargo, including weapons, from Tehran to the Syrian regime since at least 2013." https://www.treasury.gov/press-center/press-releases/pages/jl2618.aspx

8   In 2011, Iran Air and Mahan Airlines were sanctioned by the U.S. Department of Treasury for supporting Iran's Revolutionary Guard Corps and its ballistic missile program. A year later, the Treasury Department alleged that "Iran used Iran Air and Mahan Air flights between Tehran and Damascus to send military and crowd control equipment to the Syrian regime".

little solid evidence that the equipment in question would have a military use.

In 2006 and 2007, three ageing Boeing 747s found a new home in Seoul, South Korea. They had been retired by United Airlines and bought by a British company, which had somewhat murky plans for the venerable airliners.[9]

In subsequent months US officials – quoted in diplomatic cables – said they had "strong reason to believe the aircraft are intended for delivery to Iranian civil airline Mahan Air," which would violate US sanctions.

At that time, the global reach of US sanctions was both largely untested and unclear. They were certainly more ambitious – or draconian – than the sanctions against Iran introduced by Europe. For example, the US claimed what was known as extra-territorial jurisdiction over the operations of all civil aircraft that had more than 10 per cent US-made parts. The operators of such planes (which included Airbus aircraft) had to apply for a license to service certain territories, including Iran.

The Korean example is a classic case of how the US was doing the seeking, and a lot of people were doing the hiding, as the US Treasury Department upped its game.

US diplomats worked hard to ensure the Boeing 747s – which were being serviced by Korean Air – were kept on the ground. But even they had to admit that the transfer to the UK-based Balli Group *could* be in violation of US law. The planes were in the livery of a Balli subsidiary – but their operator was

---

9   N106UA and N192UA were at Incheon International, and N185UA was at Kimhae International.

listed as in the former Soviet republic of Armenia – typical of such convoluted arrangements.

US officials had seen this pattern before. Three other planes acquired by Balli had ended up in the fleet of Mahan Air, which had leased the planes from the Armenian-listed carrier Blue Airways.

The Islamic Republic used a far-flung network of Iranian expatriates to help it evade US sanctions; and the Balli Group was a typical example. Founded by Iranian-born Vahid Alaghband, Balli was based in the exclusive Mayfair neighborhood of London. Alaghband's brothers Hassan and Nasser were also on Balli's board.

Mahan Air – according to the US Treasury – had close links with the Iranian Revolutionary Guard Corps (IRGC). As one diplomatic cable put it at the time, "Given Iran's continued sponsorship of international terrorism as well as its missile program, we remain concerned about its ability to misuse civilian aircraft for nefarious activities."

The US Commerce Department was also brought to bear. Its Office of Export Enforcement hand-delivered a letter to Balli's Houston office in February 2008 requiring the planes to be delivered to the US for inspection.

But the Koreans were wary of the legitimacy of US demands. As a close ally, they wanted to help – but were not convinced the planes were on their way to Iran. Nor were they confident that they could enforce the US government's order that the planes be flown to America. A senior Korean official told US diplomats in Seoul that he was worried a press leak "that could portray the ROKG as acting on behalf of the U.S.

without any basis in international law."

The South Koreans also wanted evidence that Balli's planes had been used in contravention of existing UN sanctions. There was even discussion of trying to persuade Balli to sell the planes to a non-Iranian carrier. In addition to the game of hide-and-seek, there was a lot of arm-twisting on Washington's part.

And getting results took persistence, luck and co-operative courts. In the UK, the Treasury told its American cousins that Balli had not broken any laws. The resources of US investigations, plus some heavy duty federal legislation, frequently tipped the balance. Balli eventually paid $14.25 million in fines after pleading guilty in US court to illegally exporting aircraft to Iran.

From 2008, the United States stepped up pressure on European allies and governments elsewhere in the world to go after companies who were cutting Iranian firms some slack. Insurers, shipping lines, oil equipment and trading companies – all came in for the same treatment. It all depended on how much a government wanted to please its friends in Washington. In Britain's case, that was quite a lot. In South Africa's case, not so much. But that could always change. The National Intelligence Agency was beginning to take a closer look at dealings with Iran, and especially what it regarded as 'front companies' set up by Iranians in South Africa.

CHAPTER SEVEN

WEDDED TO CALAMITY
2009

Maybe I was gaining a local reputation as a young guy who embraced risk and was not too worried by the letter of the law. Maybe I just moved in circles where such reputations were the standard. Maybe I just attracted trouble.

Even as I was trying to keep my Iranian business alive, I was open to other opportunities; and they would come from the most unusual places.

In February 2009 my brother held a barbeque – known as a *braai* in South Africa – at his home in the Cape Town suburbs. It was a glorious summer's evening, a mild breeze taking the edge of a still fierce sun. The drinks were flowing.

My brother had collected some unusual acquaintances, guys who like the smell of a good deal, who liked to be called 'brokers' for want of a more accurate or perhaps more vernacular description.

One of them was a short, solidly-built man in his forties who would always lubricate a party with his oversize bonhomie, stock of jokes and ability to make anyone think they really were interesting.

"Ah, the little brother!" he exclaimed, a not too subtle riff on my brother's seniority and his expanding girth.

"You are the family globe-trotter, I hear. All this exotic travel – Israel, Iran……Ever go to Dubai?"

"Oh yes," I said. "It's become the hub. I'm back there next week."

"Diamonds," he continued, oblivious to the *non-sequitur*.

"I have a 5.297 carat, D, VVS2 which I sold to this old lady," he confided, lowering his voice for effect and trying to blind me with gem science.

"I made 300,000 Rand just on that sale. There are even better opportunities overseas. But I need a partner."

He let his words hang, waiting for a reaction.

An acquaintance had recently told me that I was like Jay Gatsby, someone who would always make more money outside the system than in. I was a 21st century boot-legger. My mother saw it differently. I wanted life to be a rollercoaster of risk. I was, she said, intoning Shakespeare's Romeo, "wedded to calamity."

"Always open to new possibilities," I said – knowing I could not resist them. "Send me the details and photos tomorrow."

And with that, he wandered away, turning to say – with a sly smile – "You'll be hearing from me."

At 07.00 a.m. the next morning I heard the familiar whirring of my Blackberry. My 'broker' friend had sent me the specifications of the diamonds he wanted me to sell on behalf of a client.

Three days later, I arrived in the wealthy emirate with about $500,000 worth of diamonds in my jeans pocket.

I was – to put it mildly – nervous. While Dubai is a relatively safe place, a diamond dealer had recently been murdered at the

Burj al Arab Hotel by Russian gangsters.[10] But with a helicopter business that was struggling, I needed some income – and fast.

My destination was the Bur Dubai Souk - a small, enclosed lane with shops selling gold, diamonds and platinum in every imaginable configuration. There were some seedy alleyways leading off the souk that I decided to avoid at all costs. It would not be easy to explain away a street robbery to my broker acquaintance.

The searing heat, combined with my jet lag and apprehension, made we wonder whether yet again I was in over my head.

Within a few minutes my cellphone rang.

"Mr Brendel, how are you my friend?" I said.

Brendel was a German living in Dubai and styled himself as a general commodity trader – a description that covered a multitude of sins. He wanted to get to work immediately, as I was due to fly home just 36 hours after arriving. I was already counting down the hours.

We met on the street minutes later, two pale men sweating profusely in the suffocating humidity.

Silver-haired, he might have looked distinguished in another setting. At that moment, he had the appearance of a seamy wheeler-dealer, perspiration coloring the neck and armpits of his expensive shirt.

Our odyssey through the souk began, bodyguard in tow. We weaved through small side-streets, and entered a nameless building with narrow stairs. Surely not here, I thought to myself. But exterior appearances were deceiving. On an upper

---

10   https://7starsdubai.wordpress.com/2008/01/16/members-of-gang-held-for-murder-at-dubai-hotel-burj-al-arab-2/

floor, we were greeted by a bullet-proof glass door with digital access pads. Buzzed in, another door was unlocked – and suddenly we were in the presence of a Lebanese gem dealer. He was poring over dozens of diamonds on the desk in front of him. The sight was, literally, breath-taking.

His bushy eyebrows were magnified by heavily-framed glasses as he looked up from his treasure. He didn't have a sense of humor, and was not one for pleasantries.

"What's the big guy for?" he asked in a thick Lebanese accent.

"Protection," I said abruptly, my mood deteriorating by the moment.

"Show him the stuff," Brendel ordered gruffly. I was not in the presence of charmers.

The Lebanese turned to his loupe and viewed each one carefully. He knew he held the upper hand. The global recession was kicking in, and not even wealthy Dubai was spared.

The dealer studied the gems closely, and then pushed back his chair. The moment of truth had arrived, and it was not a good moment.

He offered me 40% less than the broker's 'reserve price.'

It was not a long exchange. Rather than haggle, I was in the mood to move on. But everywhere we went in the souk, we met with the same response. Business was not good; dealers were sitting on too much supply. Even the super-rich were holding on to their cash.

Brendel could tell I was flagging.

"Let's go for dinner at my place and then we will have a very good friend of mine view the stones," he said. "He has a shop in Abu Dhabi."

Hungry, tired and getting desperate I weakly agreed. His 'place' was in an upscale expatriate enclave. We were met by his suspicious bull mastiff and his equally wary Romanian girl-friend. I felt as if I was in a David Lynch film.

An ice-cold German beer began to revive me as we sat by the pool awaiting his friend. But I knew this was our last shot.

His 'friend' was of Russian descent, which in light of recent events did not encourage me.

We were asking too much, he said with a shrug. But the broker's diamond was an interesting specimen, a 'specialty stone' he called it.

"Let me keep the stones here for a week and show them to some other buyers in Abu Dhabi," Brendel suggested.

"You'll have to call my friend," I said – suddenly elevating our relationship.

He did, proposing to write a cheque for the full value of the diamonds – as he defined it – as surety. This was acceptable, because bouncing a cheque in Dubai is a serious criminal offence.

I left the gems and walked out with a piece of paper. I didn't feel good about it, but the diamond business was new to me. Perhaps this was a quite routine arrangement.

I spent the next few days in my Cape Town office looking at the phone and checking emails as if possessed. Nothing. Except for voicemails from the short, stout broker, which became more profane with each call – all seventeen of them.

Finally, I took a call from him.

"Where are you?" he asked bluntly. No friendly party talk.

"At the office."

"I'll be there in 5 minutes."

I went down to what I grandly called the boardroom and sat down in an oversize leather chair. It squeaked ominously. How appropriate, I thought.

Minutes later, the 'broker' barged in. I had seen that expression before among members of Cape Town's mob. He was accompanied by a man built like an armored car.

"So, you know why we are here?" he began with a look of fury.

"Yes, the diamond is not back yet and the German is not replying to any calls."

"We suggest you fly to Dubai and retrieve the diamond or cash the cheque and bring us our money."

It wasn't really a suggestion.

He got up and pointed his stubby index finger at me.

"You have 72 hours."

Strangely, the encounter only served to make me furious. The very next evening I was on the Emirates flight to Dubai.

No sooner had the plane reached its gate than I switched on my phone. It was 5am.

Brendel sounded alarmed despite being incoherent with sleep.

"We can meet at your hotel in three hours," he said.

"Good, because I'm not meeting anywhere else."

He had scarcely sat down in the lobby of the airport Hilton when I leant forward – unnecessarily close to his greasy, pock-marked face.

"Now Heinz, listen to me very carefully. Where. Are. The.

Diamonds?"

I was being patronizing, aggressive. But that was the point. Unsettle him.

"Well…. with this guy."

"Which guy Heinz? Tell me the truth." The accent was very much on the word 'guy.'

"See, Heinz, this is my problem. I have the local debt collectors on my ass and you keep screwing me around. I need the diamonds. You take me to this guy now or I am going to the police and I'll get you charged with theft."

Then the lie.

"I have a very good lawyer here. He's helped put away all sorts of characters like you."

I was beginning to get some perverted pleasure from being the heavy.

"OK. We'll go find them."

'Them,' I thought. First time I'd heard a plural. Suddenly I wished I had a handgun tucked into my belt.

Two hours later, in a drab office on the souk, we were still waiting. I paced the room, recalling that just a week earlier on my first visit here I had promised myself not to end up in a place like this.

There was a knock at the door and two men of indeterminate origin sidled in. They did not look nervous. But I had to 'stay on offense' as the Americans like to say.

"So, where are my diamonds boys" I asked.

One of them broke into a broad grin, exposing discolored teeth I badly wanted to rearrange.

"Your diamonds?!" he laughed. "Seriously?"

"You can have 'your' diamonds" - he even shaped his fingers as inverted commas – "when you repay us the $100,000 Heinz borrowed."

I turned to Heinz, but he was no longer there. He had slipped out of the room like a cat burglar.

One of my new-found acquaintances said that Heinz had raised cash with the diamonds - $100,000 – so he could profit from some gold deal he had in the works. Except the deal was a scam – and the $100,000 had vanished into the Dubai haze.

I confronted Heinz with his colleagues' disclosure when he returned from his bathroom break.

"Here's what we are going to do," I said, making up the plan as I went.

"We're going to Rak Bank to deposit your cheque and then we are going to pay these nice gentlemen and then they are going to give me the diamonds."

He looked at me pathetically.

"But I don't have that kind of money in my account, I have no money," he said.

"Then you are going to jail my friend," I said.

I had to get to Rak Bank before it closed. With a thumping headache and a serious case of nausea, I arrived just in time to find out that Heinz, for once in his life, was not lying.

Rather than a six-figure sum in his account, there was a one-figure sum in his account.

Life could not get worse, but quickly did. When I arrived at the airport hotel, desperate for a shower and time to plan my next move, I received a text from my brother. The heading – URGENT – did not inspire confidence.

50

Broker called, said if u don't return with diamond or money he will have our wives raped, poison our dogs & kill us both.

I tried calling the broker; no luck. In a rage I hammered out a text.

You as much as stare in the direction of my family and you will be the one raped.

Brave words, but I had to think; I had to set aside my anger and my desperation.

Of course, there was no lawyer in Dubai, nor did I have the faintest idea how to approach the police. And unless they wrote me a cheque for $100,000 between now and the following day, their involvement would only take matters out of my hands.

The only other people I knew in Dubai were partners in a private jet company. We had come up with an ingenious business plan to market an executive jet made by the Canadian company Bombardier. They lived and breathed aviation and were as honest and straightforward as Heinz was cunning and duplicitous.

Without even calling, I went straight to their offices. They were surprised to see me and even more surprised to see my panic-stricken demeanor, no longer the chipper rugby star from South Africa.

"Guys, I have a real big problem - and the safety of my family is at risk," I began, before unburdening myself of the whole story.

The three of them stared at me as if I'd just revealed I was an Iranian agent.

I slumped back in my chair, and there was an awkward silence.

"So," said one of them, "Let's go to the bank and get you some money. Your family is worth a hell of a lot more than $100,000."

An hour later the four of us sat in an apartment with a group of Indians who had taken possession of the diamonds. Few words were exchanged. The cashier's cheque was scrutinized, the gems returned in a small velvet bag.

One of my partners in the executive jet project took me to the airport a few hours later. I was profuse in my thanks to the point of babbling.

As he escorted me into the terminal, he paused to light a cigarette.

"Glad to help, but just don't screw me over. I know it may take a while, but pay me back."

"Remember," he said grinning, "I'm Italian."

I would pay them back, and would one day prevail upon them again in even more dire circumstances.

I slept most of the way home, the sleep of redemption and relief. When I arrived I was rejuvenated and looking forward to my imminent encounter with the broker.

I tapped out his number on my phone. It went to voicemail.

"My house at 10am, or your diamond gets flushed."

He arrived at the exact appointed time, and appeared to want to explain his vicious text. I was having none of it.

I threw the little velvet bag at him, and sharing a look of venom between him and the armored car, told him to leave my property immediately.

A frisson of satisfaction ran through me; I was the master of my destiny again. But I knew I had a debt of honor to three of the very few trustworthy men I had met in my fledgling business career.

I also knew that my foray into diamond dealing had left my cash flow in a perilous state.

CHAPTER EIGHT

THE MAN FROM COLOMBO

The global recession that had even touched the Gulf was pummeling South Africa. Tourism was down and with it our core business. Other companies were seeing their planes repossessed. Neil and our other partner, Milton, left the business; they could no longer afford to keep their shriveling equity tied up.

We didn't even own our handful of helicopters; we leased them. Soon the leasing payments were outstripping revenue by some distance. The tension of staving off creditors further undermined my professional relationship with my brother, which was still smarting from our ill-fated night-club venture. I felt I was doing the lion's share of the work; weeks would pass without us speaking. Ultimately we agreed to split the business – I would handle sales and he would try to revive the tourism side.

I moved back out to the airport, to a small hangar right next to my former colleagues at Base 4. My dreams of overtaking them, my quiet reproach of their plodding progress, looked seriously misplaced now. I had $10,000 left; Munique was beginning to worry about the mortgage.

A businessman I had met years earlier had advised me to steer clear of the aviation industry.

"If you want to be worth a million dollars in aviation, start with two million," he had quipped.

Undeterred, I wanted one more attempt. I had worked hard to establish myself in the aviation industry and I was still in my twenties. There was still time to make a name for myself.

Just as my Iranian contact Hossein had found me out of nowhere, so did my next client.

It was August 15th 2010. My business was hobbling along. The emails weren't exactly flooding in. And then this:

Dear Sir,

We are looking for 2 Bell UH-1H ex-military helicopters to buy for our client. Please call XXX-XXX-XXXX

Jagesh

The Bell UH-1H - better known as the "Huey" - is a multi-purpose helicopter famous for its role in the Vietnam war, where the trademark "whomp-whomp" sound of its rotors echoed through the hills.

Beyond the military, it's used for fire-fighting and aid distribution.

It was an odd request as I hadn't advertised any for offer. The Huey didn't come on to the market very often. And it came from an odd place: Colombo, Sri Lanka.

But I could hardly pick and choose the business I wanted. I called the number.

"This is Barry from 360 Aviation, you sent an enquiry regarding the sale of UH-1's?"

"Hold please Sir" replied the Sri Lankan accent.

The next accent was very different, very British.

"This is Luke Miller. Hello Barry; thanks for calling."

There was no pause.

"I'm looking for two or three UH-1H helicopters," he said,

as if ordering a cheeseburger.

"Well, I can begin to look; I am sure I can source them from somewhere," I said with a confident tone.

Mr Miller said he had a UN contract in Sudan. For some reason I didn't believe him, nor did I believe his real name was Miller.

"And I need some other equipment. You might describe it as more sensitive. You will receive an email within 24 hours. Let me know if you can help. Obviously any communications between us must be in absolute confidence."

Where had he found me? What on earth did he want?

The answer was soon in my inbox; not so much helicopter parts as the weapons to shoot them down. In fact, a shopping list for a small army. I still have the email:

See attached list, can you source these items? We need them ASAP and delivery we will arrange. Have you been able to get us options on the helicopters?

SA16 GIMLET IGLA 9M313-1 - LAUNCHER 9P519

KONKURS (LAUNCHER 9P 135 with Missile 9M 113)

Motor Sich MS 400 engine for UAV/Tactical Cruise Missile - 85kg dry weight

Kornet - E Anti Tank Missiles & Launchers

Krasnapol - MKM1 155mm Laser Guided Missiles

I should have just deleted the mail, not least because it looked like the sort of list to instigate a coup or arm a guerrilla group. I also had no idea how to get hold of such weapons.

There again, I was 'wedded to calamity' and I wanted to expand my network of contacts. Just because something is highly unusual doesn't mean it's illegal, I said to myself. And

I did know someone who could shed some light on such a request.

Jean-Jacques Savaulere* sold weapons for a living. He was a legitimate dealer; everything he sourced and sold had a proper end-user's certificate. I had met him at the Paris Air Show when discussing an aircraft purchase with a client. We had enjoyed each other's company.

"As long as there are wars, there will be arms dealers," he had told me unapologetically. "Global conflict and terrorism are everywhere, and while it's sad to say, they are a part of our daily lives."

Maybe Jean-Jacques could tell me something about Luke Miller or explain the meaning of his shopping list. The word 'missile' suggested something other than target practice.

Mr Miller himself was quite the Pimpernel, continuously travelling, a new mobile number every week. But wherever he was, he had time to add to his shopping list – asking for quotes immediately on obscure items that might fit on a helicopter or be launched from a tube. And he also wanted airfreight quotations to some pretty exotic destinations: Damascus, Syria; Isfahan, Iran; Baghdad and even somewhere called Landi Kotal in Pakistan.

The most frequent item on his lists was the ubiquitous Kalashnikov rifle, the calling card of guerrilla groups and terrorist cells everywhere. But the Russian made AK-47 was also in demand with governments, some of which would pass the weapon on to their favorite insurgency.

Its slick composite of forged steel and plywood makes the AK-47 deadly, but at nine pounds it is relatively light for a firearm. It doesn't jam, break or overheat. And it is cheaper than any western gun that serves the function.

I managed to help Miller buy and transport a few of the things he wanted, though none of the more exotic equipment. And we stayed in touch. It was a haphazard long-distance relationship almost exclusively carried out on email. But very soon it would be of great interest to some new partners I was about to meet.

CHAPTER NINE

HERE BE DRAGONS
2010-11

By the middle of 2010, things were beginning to look up. I had kept up my contacts in Iran, despite the often tortuous nature of the negotiations, and as other countries began to apply stricter interpretations of sanctions or introduce their own, my contacts in Tehran came to see South Africa as a safe-haven.

I felt my business was secure and with good management and fewer rash decisions could grow. I had learned a lot of different lessons in a lot of different countries – some of them painful, some of them costly. Few had enhanced my view of human nature. But I was more mature for the experience.

It helped that money could buy anything in South Africa, especially those with political power or influence. Nelson Mandela's departure from the political stage had put an end to moderation or self-restraint. With the right amount deposited into an offshore account, almost anything was possible.

The thing about corrupt politicians is they are usually in politics for nothing more than to accumulate power and money, and to hell with those plebs who were stupid enough to vote for them.

They arrange their slice of the "take" in companies they're supporting, by appointing spouses or close family as board members or holders of equity instruments and money stock options. If it all gets a bit too hot for them to operate or they decide they've had enough of politics, they'll retire as non-executive directors of the boards of their client companies.

Corruption, not merit, will often determine who wins and who loses out, who gets rich and who doesn't. For centuries, corruption has created enclaves of poverty by diverting resources to one place and not another. And it happens all over the world, not just in South Africa. Corruption isn't just about cash. Everywhere in the world, and every day, corrupt officials pedal advantage, status and opportunity in exchange for cash.

The corruption in South Africa, or anywhere actually, is not about people from different cities, states, countries or continents, but rather about people in general. Although corruption is often about "good and evil," my experience in intelligence and counter intelligence work has shown me it's usually much more complicated than that.

Politicians who hold themselves out as standard bearers of democracy deserve this scrutiny because it creates space to be filled by better, more capable people. It is what drives the standard of elected officials up and makes way for stronger, smarter people who can perform better and make better choices under pressure. People who, like Nelson Mandela can put others before themselves, and make decisions for the good of everyone, not just for personal gain.

This is where sanctions busting comes in, because within the Iranian deals, international sanctions soon became a political chip to be horse-traded and used to create personal wealth and illicit advantage for deeply undeserving benefactors, people who were prepared to use the political process as a means to an end—the acquisition of personal wealth, whatever the consequences. The democratic process is, for them, artificial—a mere *fait accompli* signed, sealed and delivered before any vote gets cast.

Moreover, these people don't respect the people who elect them—the honest voters who cast their vote trusting that politicians will do honest work, with public service in mind, while paying attention to basic, universal principles of justice, decency and respect we all recognize, whatever our level of education or intellect.

Aside from an absence of integrity, many other things didn't matter in the sanctions busting horse trade. One was the implications of disregarding international sanctions on the world stage, which has created a more militarily capable Iran.

This, in turn, has led to terrorists, the world over, armed to the teeth with U.S. technologies and weapons, whatever their cause or aims. U.S. put weapons and technologies in the hands of enemies including ISIS and Al Qaeda. U.S. soldiers and interests were attacked, murdered and maimed with their own weapons. This provides more traction for black markets pedaling products whether they are harmful, poisonous or defective. Black markets enrich and empower. This is what happens when respect for international sanctions becomes a bargaining chip to be laid on the table; lost and won, bought and sold.

Enter Raisaka Masebelanga, part of the South Africa power elite. They are the most important people in South

Africa because of their access to the right networks, ability to influence outcomes, their wealth or their ability to help others create massive wealth.

An eloquent lawyer once well-placed within the ruling African National Congress, Raisaka had an agile mind and his hand-tailored suits and silk ties evidenced expensive tastes.

My first encounter with him was when the state airline, the notoriously inefficient South African Airways, wanted to dispose of its fleet of leased Boeing 747s. We wanted the contract and Raisaka was the man we contacted to make a pitch to the board.

That bid didn't win, but I kept in touch with him. We would meet whenever he was in Cape Town, and he came to our launch of the Africa franchise for the much sought-after Phoenix CJR business jet. He was a useful man to know.

So when the National Iranian Oil Company invited my little outfit to tender for a big order of helicopters and helicopter parts, my first call was to Raisaka. The question was simple: could he help with export permissions if we won the bid?

This was no routine order; it could amount to $100 million in machinery. We would need serious backing from the Department of Trade, and it would probably be referred all the way up to the President's office – given that such a deal would hardly escape the Americans' notice.

Raisaka was interested. He could smell profit, even down a phone line. I imagined him placing a call to his tailor after hanging up.

Business was good enough for me to take Munique to the island of Phuket in Thailand for a New Year's celebration. We had just returned, and I was clearing the backlog of emails when my Blackberry buzzed. I will never forget the fateful date: 19th January 2011.

'Unknown Number' illuminated the screen, the sort of lack of information that infuriated me. It could either be someone selling credit cards from a high-tech sweatshop in Bangalore or my most valuable client ever.

"Hello."

"Can I speak with Mr Barend Oberholzer," intoned a very American female.

There was something about her voice that made me sit up. She was not selling.

"This is me."

"Hi – my name is Kerry Jones.[11] I'm with the U.S. Embassy in Pretoria, and we'd like to set up a meeting with you."

"Yes. Ma'am, I'm available anytime this week," I replied as casually as possible. I didn't even ask why she wanted to meet; we shared an unspoken assumption.

"Thank you. Please meet me at the U.S. Consulate in Cape Town, Friday at 11 a.m."

It was not a consular services courtesy call. I was both intrigued and a little apprehensive. As a US citizen, I was obviously subject to US law and some of my business ventures – the good, the bad and the ugly – had probably veered beyond the limits of federal legislation.

My unease was not misplaced.

*

---

11   The names of US officials involved in intelligence work have been changed.

"I'm here to see Kerry Jones," I told the receptionist at the consulate, after going through the sort of security I would have expected at Langley.

A consular official greeted me with a firm handshake.

"Mr. Oberholzer, thank you for coming. Follow me please."

He escorted me to yet another security check, where I had to give up my phone. I was not about to be asked to run an expats' bingo night.

Guided toward an inner sanctum, I was stunned to see lush rolling lawns, benches next to paved walkways that meandered under manicured trees. This probably didn't qualify as a hardship post in the US Diplomatic Service.

My guide was courteous, and the surroundings more like a Club Med than a Consulate. But I couldn't escape visions of being strapped to a polygraph machine in a windowless room and asked a hundred questions about Iran.

In fact, I was met by a well-dressed woman in her mid-forties with a business-like hairstyle and what I would call 'sensible' shoes.

She smiled and thanked me for coming – perhaps everyone would – but did not introduce herself. Instead she led me into a bland office space where another woman, much younger and with flowing blond hair, was sitting – notepad at the ready.

She was one of those young women whose attractiveness is enhanced by the way they wear glasses, and the way she deftly slipped them off was like a facial striptease.

"This is my associate," said Ms Sensible Shoes. Clearly no-one had a name around here.

"Coffee? Tea?"

I resisted the temptation to ask for a large Scotch.

There was no foreplay.

The younger woman started business.

"We are interested in your dealings in Iran. Please elaborate further on the companies you are dealing with as well as names of individuals."

The questioning went on for two hours. At no point did either of the women suggest I had broken any laws. They didn't need to. But in a methodical, almost fastidious way, they vacuumed up every last detail of my contacts with Iranians, official and otherwise.

At the end of it all, the younger woman removed her glasses again.

"We very much appreciate you coming here, and we will be in touch again."

It didn't sound like a threat, and perhaps it wasn't. Perhaps it was a warning – that I was sailing close to the wind and that their future dispensation towards me would entirely depend on how willing I was to co-operate.

On the drive home, I re-ran the conversation a dozen times. Had I been forthright enough? Had my recollections been accurate?

What I didn't know was the fine print of United Nations Security Council resolution 9948, drafted by the US and passed a few months previously. In response to Iran's continuing obstruction of international inspections of its nuclear facilities, the Security Council had widened sanctions – mandatory for all member states.

The critical paragraph stipulated "that all States shall prevent the direct or indirect supply, sale or transfer to Iran, from or through their territories or by their nationals or individuals subject to their jurisdiction, or using their flag vessels or aircraft, and whether or not originating in their territories, of any battle tanks, armored combat vehicles, large caliber artillery systems, combat aircraft, attack helicopters, warships, missiles or missile systems as defined for the purpose of the United Nations Register of Conventional Arms, or related materiel, including spare parts."[12]

My shipping of a Bell 212 to Valadkhani had been concluded before the passage of the UN resolution, but I had been operating in a grey area and I knew the federal government could make my life very difficult if it chose to.

As a precaution I began to gather as much information as I could over the next few days: emails, invoices, contact numbers, business cards and addresses, even hotel bills to prove the dates I had been in Tehran. I also put together a paper on the projects and products in which my contacts were most interested.

A flurry of secure email traffic followed. I told my new friends that an Iranian broker was interested in the delivery of five aircraft and related equipment. A bank account in Azerbaijan would be of considerable interest, I said. Then there was an order for 200 Ballistic Protection Jackets from the Iran Investment Company.

I also recalled my contacts with Koorush Taherkhani, the brains behind a front company based in Dubai that trawled

---

12   http://www.un.org/press/en/2010/sc9948.doc.htm

for high-tech military equipment in the US and beyond. Taherkhani's activities were of great interest to my US handlers, as they began to investigate the activities of his company – TIG Marine. Within a few months, they began to find out just how serious and ambitious a player Taherkhani was.

I wanted to show my contacts at the embassy that I had some serious clients. But I also broached the subject of payment. I was about to destroy a business I had spent three years building up; and a lot of relationships. There had to be some *quid pro quo*.

And then fate paid a visit, in the form of a call from Raisaka Masebelanga. He'd been investigating the possibility of high-level support for the deal with the National Iranian Oil Corporation. When I had mentioned the possibility to my interrogators at the Consulate, there had been more than a frisson of interest.

"We'll be ready in two weeks," he said. "How's February 17th?"

I checked my calendar.

"That's great," I said.

It was a watershed moment. I was either 'all in' with the US government, or I had to shelve the whole NIOC project and retreat into the shadows.

Since when had I embraced retreat?

Within 15 minutes of hanging up with Raisaka, I was tapping out a text to Kerry Jones.

Need to meet. Have urgent update.

Sure. Tuesday? Pretoria?

*

The US Embassy in Pretoria is not a thing of beauty unless you like functional modern architecture. A bland, unwelcoming structure that could have been a children's spaceship design. And as always in the age of truck bombs, the buildings were set well back from the road that runs through the diplomatic enclave in Hatfield.

I started the multi-layered security procedures at the outside gate.

"I'm here to see the Regional Security Officer," I told the unsmiling officer, following Kerry's instructions.

She was keen to disguise the real purpose of my visit now that the stakes were getting higher.

'Say you are here for an American Citizens Services visit,' she had told me in an email.

The RSO was out of central casting – broad-shouldered with a buzz cut and square cheekbones. In fact, everything about him seemed square.

I was ushered upstairs and taken to a windowless room that looked like a makeshift break room rather than an office.

Kerry was more welcoming this time.

"Hi Barry, thanks for coming, grab a seat. This is Carl Edwards," she said – gesturing to a man who could have been the RSO's older – and shorter - brother. Edwards had a serious but not unwelcoming expression.

"Hello, Barry – good to meet you." He fixed me with his pale blue eyes and shook my hand, before reaching into his wallet for a business card.

Carl Edwards, Legal Attache

FBI, I thought. It was the way they dressed up their

expanding presence in diplomatic missions.

"Carl is here in his capacity as Legal Attache as we, the CIA, have a jurisdiction issue with your dual nationality," Kerry said. It sounded ominous.

"As a US citizen, you fall under the FBI. We as the CIA will work in a supportive role," she added.

I wondered if they enjoyed supporting each other or spent most of their working lives trying to keep secrets from each other. The rivalries were famous but to an extent had been eroded by the post 9/11 world and the need to cooperate in the battle against international terrorism.

Carl cleared his throat.

"Kerry has briefed me about your situation and I have also read your report and sent it to the folks back home."

"You certainly have information of interest. Is there a possibility of you relocating to the US so that you can continue working with us or is your intention to stay in South Africa?"

I wasn't expecting such a dramatic opening gambit, but Munique and I had been talking about moving to the US. She was pregnant with our first child, Chloe.

I didn't want to sound too enthusiastic.

"I think I'd be willing to move if necessary." I replied.

"Any thought of where?"

"Probably Los Angeles."

I had travelled widely in the West Coast and always loved southern California – the coastline, the mountains and the desert. And the climate wasn't that dissimilar to Cape Town. I couldn't have coped with Minnesota.

"You like to sit in traffic then?" Carl said, trying to break the ice.

Always businesslike, Kerry took up the reins.

"So, you said there is something important coming up?"

"Yes. One of the people I am working with has set up a meeting with a "high level delegation" where we will discuss gaining support for the NIOC tender. My contact mentioned these people are close to "Number One", which I took to mean the President of South Africa."

"Well that's interesting. But," and here came the 'CIA' moment, "under no circumstances are we instructing you to obtain information as an instruction from the U.S. government."

She was waiting on what's known as an OIA ('otherwise illegal activity') which authorizes a confidential informant to engage in activities that would otherwise constitute crimes.

The vetting process is necessarily rigorous – or all sorts of nefarious types would be traipsing into US diplomatic missions the world over.

"I'll let you know when the meeting is confirmed and come by afterwards," I offered.

As I walked out of the embassy, I was enveloped by a feeling of deep apprehension. Beyond the veneer of excitement at being involved – however obliquely – in the world of espionage, I was beginning to realize that I had very little protection should things go wrong. You crossed South Africa's new elite at your peril. They were not beyond manipulating the justice system for their own ends, nor more severe retaliation for anyone who might style themselves a 'whistleblower.'

And I wasn't sure I could carry off the 'double-life' that I would have to lead. Telling simple truths would be unceremoniously jettisoned in exchange for a farrago of lies that would grow ever more complex. The risk of discovery would haunt me night and day. And it wasn't just the South African power-brokers I would have to worry about; the Islamic Republic would be none too happy to have one of its favorite sanctions-busting routes sabotaged. And its more militant factions were known to have carried out plenty of assassinations overseas.

As I boarded the plane home, I wrestled with a lot of choices. How much to tell Munique? How much to demand of the Americans in the way of protection and assurances? How deep to travel into this unforgiving world?

CHAPTER TEN

MAMA GUGU
February 2011

The restaurant at the Ten Bompas hotel in Johannesburg was the watering hole of South Africa's power-brokers – plush, wildly expensive but with a number of private dining areas where deals could be struck beyond flapping ears.

It was the venue chosen by Raisaka to open contacts about helping get 'lift-off' for the massive NIOC deal.

The morning of February 17th 2011 I compulsively checked my Blackberry to ensure it was fully charged. The days of Charlie Sheen being 'wired' in the movie Wall Street were long gone. Now you just needed a discreetly placed smartphone.

I arrived about 20 minutes early and texted Raisaka.

"We need to meet privately before they arrive."

He arrived as if straight from the drycleaners, everything perfectly pressed. He wore a broad smile as he walked towards me, perhaps seeing me as a stack of $100 bills.

He gave me a quick briefing on how he expected the meeting to unfold and told me to let him do the talking.

'Be my guest,' I thought, praying I had hit Record and not Play.

Within a few minutes, Joe Mboweni bounded up the steps and into the reception area. Mboweni was a Johannesburg businessman and confidant of President Jacob Zuma. He usually got what he wanted.

The conceit was not that complicated. We would set up a company in South Africa that would win the contract to supply helicopters – mostly US-made – to the National Iranian Oil Corporation, or at least ostensibly the NIOC. Those who helped facilitate the contract and the export permissions would be suitably rewarded.

"We are still waiting for Mama, she will be here soon," Mboweni said.

Mama was the universal nickname for the girlfriend of Deputy President Kgalema Motlanthe. She also normally got what she wanted. Her imperious bearing as she entered the room in a loose-fitting dress of swirling, vivid colors, suggested she did not suffer fools.

The private dining room was an intimate space where waiters hovered in the background. The table was covered in starched linen; polished wine glasses reflected the colorful borders of shrubs beyond the picture window. Delicate chandeliers made of blue glass lotus leaves floated above.

Raisaka introduced me to everyone and said I was one of South Africa's most promising entrepreneurs – with a unique proposition. He extended his palm, which I imagined he did a great deal, and asked me to explain.

I looked at each one of the assembled company. They were hungry.

"The contract is $60 million per year of revenue," I said – glancing at Mama.

"Forty percent of that would go to the newly-formed company. My company can't do this deal on our own because the letter we received from Iqbal at the DTI has expired."

I could almost hear them calculating 40 per cent of $60 million.

"I don't have any other avenues at the DTI to support my venture. We will need high level support."

Raisaka interceded.

"The last time you and I talked you said there will be a commission for getting that letter."

He turned to Mboweni and explained that in return for a letter of support from the government, a commission would be paid - along with shares in my company – to those invested in the new company.

"So I just want to lay this out, if it meets your interest, Joe."

"Obviously, but I work on instruction from Mama," Mboweni said.

Gugu took a sip of water and corrected him.

"No, Joe will be instructing," she said.

"Whatever Mama instructs me to do I will do," he said.

It was an almost comical moment.

Joe was already thinking beyond this deal. There seemed no limit to the greed.

"The opportunities in aviation in Iran are big; there are also opportunities in aviation in the Congo. You said you do cargo?"

"Yes," I said.

"We have been talking to Kenya. Aquarius Aviation who used to do their cargo, the Kenyan government and aviation people were not looked after."

He leaned back.

"Whatever my leaders instruct me to do, I will do," he repeated with mock humility.

Why not go for broke, I thought? Match their ambition, make them salivate.

"There is not only aviation on the table," I said. "Also, my business partners in Iran are high level officials and former members of Parliament now living in Dubai and London. They are setting up front companies…..to supply the oil rigs with the spare parts. So it's not limited to aviation. It's oil and gas that drives…"

"Yes, sanction-busting," Mboweni interrupted.

An awkward moment of silence descended on the room, as if the truth that doth not speak its name had just been spray-painted on the wall.

"I have been there three or four times in the last three years and there are a lot of opportunities we can discuss," I said.

I had even been invited by President Thabo Mbeki to be part of his delegation on a visit to Tehran that was cancelled when he stepped down.

"We are the only company which has proved to the Iranian regime that we are capable of supplying them with aircraft and spare parts. It has taken me three years, three helicopters, and three aircraft to show that we can do it through South Africa."

*

"It's yours, take it."

Forty minutes after leaving the power-brokers' lunch I was at the US embassy, offering a small but explosive gift to Kerry.

It was a USB stick with the whole conversation.

"I have to follow procedure so we need to buy it from you,"

she said. It seemed an almost surreal detail after the agony of recording surreptitiously for two hours

"Seriously? I paid like 100 Rand for it, don't worry."

"Unfortunately, I do need to document it, let me get the paperwork and your cash quickly."

Carl and I chatted about my prospective move to Los Angeles and the various agencies that might want to meet me. There were quite a few.

"You've been very busy for someone so young," he said – half in admonition and half in admiration.

Kerry returned with my 100 Rand, which I had to sign for.

As I got up to leave, she looked at me in a more sympathetic way.

"Be safe, Barry; we look forward to working with you."

I didn't know whether to feel reassured or alarmed.

Within weeks, I was invited to a Cape Town restaurant to meet three FBI agents. They were lurking in a semi-private area at the back. I felt like I was walking into a scene from *The Godfather* and half-expected Marlon Brando to emerge from the men's room.

I was about to meet my handlers. Paul was with the Consulate in Cape Town. Originally from Miami, he would not have been out of place in a South Beach bar – a gregarious and surprisingly irreverent guy for an FBI agent.

The other two had come all the way from Los Angeles. Either a monstrous waste of taxpayers' money, I thought, or I must be more useful than I had imagined.

Nikki was petite with mouse-brown hair down to her shoulders. I imagined she was tougher than she looked. Warren was heavy-set with a goatee and must have played college football. I imagined he was as tough as he looked.

"Sorry for taking this long to get everything verified," said Nikki as we sat down. "As you know, we need to do things properly and the bureaucratic and verification process does take some time."

The reports I had handed to Kerry and Carl, replete with passport details, bank account numbers and details on what the Iranians were fishing for, had made their way to LA.

"We certainly look forward working through all this information with you," Nikki said.

They offered me no guarantees apart from help with relocating, visa assistance for Munique and the safety of my family. I didn't care about the first; the second and third were non-negotiable. I was about to become a father.

We agreed to meet in L.A. a few weeks later so that we could finalize my relocation.

I was very much Uncle Sam's man.

CHAPTER ELEVEN

THE PERSIAN PLAYBOY

I found myself living on airplanes between the Middle East and South Africa. Meeting Iranian clients based in Dubai, gathering as much intelligence as possible on their requests, often meeting into the early hours of the morning, just to check out again the following day and fly back to South Africa.

As one of these Emirates flights approached Dubai International Airport, I looked out the window as the plane's shadow was racing across the new developments popping up on the outskirts of the airport zone. I was about to meet a major role player in a sanction busting racket that went way beyond dual use goods, for his requests, there were only one use, military.

He was among the most ambitious of my Iranian contacts. Koorush Taherkhani.

An entrepreneur with a flair for running obscure front companies and links with the Revolutionary Guards. As word had spread about the young resourceful South African ready to help find essential equipment, I began correspondence with him after being introduced by a Bahraini banker.

I was surprised by his demands: there was no 'dual use' interpretation when it came to Night Vision Goggles, parts for missile development and parts for the Iranian Air Force's venerable fleet of F-4 Phantom jets.

We were sitting at an Iranian restaurant in the Dubai Mall with his German partner Mr. Ergun Yildiz, discussing their procurement needs.

Taherkhani was a powerful man, in his late thirties, whose thick black hair sprang from his arms, nose and ears. He had a jet black mane and somewhat oversized nose. He was domineering, impetuous, passionate and full of boundless self-confidence. He looked like a man with the right and power to command respect. The political climate at the time provided the much venerated Taherkhani with a new, complex arena in which he would receive even greater acclaim with his Revolutionary Guard comrades.

"Ergun here is my local partner, we do all deals together. He also travels on my behalf as I don't want to travel to places where I might be at risk.," Taherkhani said officiously.

Taherkhani had set up what might be called a 'procurement network' using a company called TIG Marine, based in Dubai.

He was TIG's founder and managing director, but its public face was a German national of Turkish heritage called Ergun Yildiz, who was President and CEO of the company. It was a classic arrangement to kick over the traces of any Iranian association.

Taherkhani was a player in a game where a decreasing number of participants were willing to take the risks. He would use his increase market power to negotiate steep premiums with his comrades in Iran. The tougher the legislators, enforcers and regulators are in cracking down, the more he had his comrades over a barrel.

He continued, "Barry, we need night vision goggles. Lots

79

of them. Can you get them? They must be American made. We also need all these helicopter and aircraft parts."

He handed me a list of items. Most were parts for the military F-4 fighter jet as well as gyro-compasses.

"We will pay good money. Please get them for us—we are desperate. Those lying American bastards, we are not wanting to bomb the world, why can't we get their equipment like they share with the Israeli's?" he pleaded, as he started a rant on the sanctions and his conspiracy theories on the American system and how they are screwing the world. He was quite a character.

Taherkhani used TIG Marine to go shopping in the United States. It helped a little that an old college friend - Arash Ghahreman – had moved to the US in 2007, just as I was looking for business in Tehran. Ghahreman was now living in Staten Island, New York. It also helped that both were graduates in marine engineering and had worked for various Iranian shipping lines.

Ghahreman had become a naturalized US citizen. With his skills and his US passport, he was the perfect scout for TIG Marine.

But Taherkhani – like so many of his peers – always had more than one line open in his efforts to source sensitive equipment. Hence the flow of emails back and forth with me. Three years after he first reached out to me, the relationship would take on a whole new meaning.

Upon my return to my hotel, I emailed my contacts at the Defense Criminal Investigation Service and briefed them on the meeting, the product requests and sent through a copy of his passport.

He had become the target of a complex and slow-burning sting operation run by Homeland Security Investigations and the Defense Criminal Investigative Service.

Beginning at the end of 2012, Taherkhani and his US agent Arash Ghahreman were drawn into a web of emails, phone calls and face-to-face meetings with undercover agents who professed to have fiber-optic gyrocompasses, electron tubes and other technology for illegal export to Iran.

Ghahreman and his TIG sponsors agreed to buy four Navigat-2100 fiber-optic gyrocompasses and fifty Y-690 electron tubes. They wired $60,000 in part-payment to a bank in the US used by the agents.[13]

On June 17 2013, federal agents arrested Ghahreman and TIG's CEO Ergun Yildiz as they took delivery of one gyrocompass and two electron tubes in San Diego and attempted to ship them to Iran, via third countries. Ghahreman was later sentenced to a six-and-a-half-year jail sentence by federal court in California.

Taherkhani was sentenced in absentia. I followed the case closely, glad that I had had a part in putting him out of business.

---

13   http://www.investigativeproject.org/case/707/us-v-ghahreman-et-al

CHAPTER TWELVE

SUNSET BOULEVARD
February 2011

"Ladies and Gentlemen, welcome to Los Angeles International Airport. The local time is 3:05 PM and the outside temperature is 80 degrees Fahrenheit..."

Emirates 215 was on its way to the stand after a seemingly endless 16-hour flight from Dubai. I should have been beyond exhaustion, but I was both excited and apprehensive. This relationship had to work.

Kerry had written encouraging words in the hours before I left Johannesburg.

"I think they will see what we saw here; that you have something valuable to offer....as always, NO GUARANTEES from my guys...That said, others have interest."

She also warned me that there might be someone waiting to meet me at the customs area and that I might be discreetly pulled aside. They would have a long wait. This was LAX, as it's universally known, quite incapable of dealing with the 75 million passengers that touch down every year. The line through Customs and Border Protection snaked back well over 200 yards. I groaned inwardly.

By the time I reached the baggage carousel, my initial frisson of adrenalin had worn off. My eyes felt as if full of sand; my body ached.

"So, how are you doing?"

I turned – momentarily disorientated.

The guy looked Italian. He was dressed in a navy windbreaker and jeans.

"I have a phone and charger with me, meeting is at 6pm, the last dialed number is *their* number. Meet them for dinner at TGI Fridays, Woodland Hills.

He looked at me.

"If you are too jetlagged, we can always change the meeting."

He slipped the phone into my jacket pocket and was gone.

After a few precious hours of sleep, I awoke in a fog of incomprehension, my brain scrambling to work out where it was and whether the sun was rising or setting.

Nikki and Warren were tucked into a corner at TGIF. These people really liked their corners.

"Things are moving along nicely on our side," said Nikki, more relaxed on home turf.

"Tomorrow we'll sort you out with some finances and then debrief some more on the information you provided."

For now, they wanted to get to know me, probably on the alert for any contradictions or inconsistencies in my story or peculiar character traits. Over dinner, the conversation ranged from sports to music and family.

As we left, Nikki said: "Do you know the Getty Center?"

Art and culture was never my strongest suit.

"Let's go tomorrow," she said. "You'll enjoy it."

Its position was spectacular, like a Crusaders' castle but overlooking the freeway and Bel Air estates. Beyond was the

Pacific Ocean, rippling and infinite. Behind, the San Gabriel Mountains.

Within the curving walls of the Center were elegant galleries and some of the world's priceless art. But I'd not paid much attention at PRG in art history classes, and soon glazed over as we passed one masterpiece after another. My new-found friends were clearly trying to be sociable and to impress me with the cultural glories around LA. But I was jaded by travel and impatient to do some business.

Eventually we sat around a table in a corner of the Center's restaurant, and *sotto voce* I ran through some of the deals that were in the pipeline.

In the midst of the Arab Spring, the regime of Bashar al Assad in Syria was beginning to shop for riot control equipment and weapons. Tehran was ready to oblige. There were parts on order for Iranian nuclear power plants, and aircraft sought by Iranian front companies.

I certainly had their attention. There was a lot of scribbling in notebooks.

"We'd like to start you off with some cash to get settled," Nikki said as we stepped out into the bright sunshine.

I followed them to the underground parking deck and a Chevrolet with tinted windows. I climbed into the back seat, and waited in the gloom.

Nikki took out an envelope, opened it, and there it was: $10,000 in fresh $100 notes. And then she set out the ritual.

"We are going to count it, then you will sign the receipt under your alias confirming you know these funds are taxable, then we will counter-sign and you will be good to go."

"And your alias from now on is Morrison."

I didn't feel like being flippant and demanding a different name, though Morrison wasn't exactly *me*.

As we parted, Warren put his hand on my shoulder.

"Remember, you are doing a good thing here. Keep your head down and your ears open."

Before I left L.A., I had a parting gift for my handlers in the shape of Mr. Luke Miller, who would quickly become a 'person of interest' to my new colleagues.

I was lucky enough, if that's the right expression, to receive a rare call from him while I was in California.

He had not become any more subtle or discreet.

"Barry!" he exclaimed with a synthetic bonhomie.

"I hope L.A. is treating you well." Seven words of small-talk: a record.

"You're going to get an email from a Lieutenant Colonel in Ivory Coast. It's urgent. Really need your help on this one."

Ivory Coast had been plunged into a spasm of political violence after a disputed election in November 2010. The opposition candidate, Alassane Ouattara, had been widely seen as the victor – by the United Nations and international observers. President Laurent Gbagbo had refused to step down, and both sides were preparing for conflict.

By early February, Ouattara's supporters had begun taking towns in the north. Ivory Coast was on the verge of its second civil war in a decade.

Within hours of Miller's call, a long email had arrived from West Africa. It was not an exercise in subterfuge but shockingly candid.

"We will need your assistance to help negotiate on my behalf purchase of aircrafts urgently needed for logistics in a plot to overthrow the incumbent president Mr. Laurent Gbagbo in my country Ivory Coast.

As you may know he have lost the election by popular vote and have refused to hand over power to the president elect Mr. Alassane Ouattara.

Perfect arrangements have been made to unsit him but as serving top military personels and our sensitive office in the government we are incapacitated to proceed for purchase of needed equipments, therefore, we decided to contact to seek your assistance.

It does not matter whether you deal on military aircrafts or not, all we need is your one-off help to secure what we need. Just a one-off help or link us with someone that will do and we will pay.

The shopping list was expansive and expensive. Assault helicopters, transport planes and what Colonel Honsou called a fast attack plane.

He listed the makes they wanted: US Hercules transport planes, Sikorsky helicopters, Sukhoi and MiGs.

A total of $60 million is budgeted for this task out of which $3 million is earmarked as your take home for your assistance.

Note that this is urgent! Please get back to us quickly, we are working on a tight schedule. [14]

I responded, asking the good Colonel who had referred him to me, and aware Miller was using the alias Travis for this deal.

He confirmed that Travis had made the connection and assumed I had contacts with organizations in Russia and Belarus that could furnish some of the planes required.

---

14   There was an intriguing footnote at the end of Colonel Honsou's email: "Afterwards we can discuss the requirement for our other export to our brothers in the Middle east."

....Please let's deal with the Russians or Belarus. Both yourself and Mr. Travis is promised a monetary compensation once we are through. Please go ahead and delete all our correspondences and please do not discuss this matter.

Nikki will enjoy this one, I thought. I set out the background of my long-distance acquaintance with Miller and presented her with the latest email exchange.

"We'd better get this to another agency," Nikki said. "Keep him warm, but make no promises."

Obviously, I thought to myself.

I strung the Colonel along; the deal was always just around the corner. His comrades were clearly working other channels, but the US was watching the Belarus connection with close interest. It was a country where companies connected with corrupt officials were feeding plenty of weapons into the illicit weapons market.

Within weeks – at the end of February 2011, the United Nations Secretary General was expressing indignation about a "serious violation" of the arms embargo by Belarus amid the violent power struggle in Ivory Coast.

One helicopter, a variant of the Russian-made Mi-24 gunship armed with machine guns and rockets, had already been delivered to opposition forces; two more were on their way. My information may have helped close one avenue for evading the embargo. Sadly, it was not the only one, and the flow of weapons from abroad would contribute to a rapidly rising death toll in Ivory Coast.

*

The next time I touched down at LAX – two months later - Munique was at my side. Our four dogs were beneath us in the hold. Our departure from South Africa had been a scramble. Munique would soon be too heavily pregnant to fly, and I felt a pressing need to consolidate and accelerate my new relationship with the federal government.

The FBI had found us a short-term apartment in Hollywood Hills. It was green, quiet and within one loud guitar riff of the Hollywood Bowl. The residences were in that Mexican style, with undulating clay-tiled roofs, so beloved of southern California.

Munique had no experience of the United States and found the scale and speed of LA unnerving. I fussed over providing every last thing she needed, anxious to make the place less intimidating.

We'd scarcely begun to unpack when Nikki called. Could I meet for breakfast at The Griddle the next morning?

Little did I know that The Griddle was a breakfast institution on Sunset Boulevard, where piles of waffles like haystacks would land every 30 seconds amid a hubbub of conversation and clinking coffee cups. Even at 7:30am the place was heaving.

All humanity was inside – groggy Japanese tourists dealing with jetlag and the American diet, a guy with a Mohawk haircut that defied gravity, a gaggle of church-going ladies with blue-rinsed hair and carefully-placed bonnets.

Piles of pancakes dripping in chocolate sauce passed by. No wonder America had an issue with obesity.

"Get used to it," teased Nikki, as I watched the towering carbohydrate rich delicacies pass me by with amazement. "We'll have to meet at different locations every week. You can't come to our offices, nor tell anyone that you are working with us, apart from your wife."

"And the dogs," I added in an effort to add some levity.

We kept things general at that first meeting: procedures rather than case details, even if it was unlikely that a teenager with a Mohawk was an informant for the Islamic Republic.

I began to find out how difficult it was to establish an identity in the US. Potential landlords wanted credit histories and any amount of detail to establish my credentials.

Most of the initial $10,000 had disappeared in moving us from South Africa, and federal bureaucracy had held up the second instalment. We were within two days of being evicted from our first apartment. We had found a better place but couldn't afford the first instalment of rent. The tension was not helping Munique.

The burner phone I'd been given by the agent at the airport rang.

"Hi, it's me," said Nikki. "We have your money; can you meet us at Roxbury Park?

The silver Chevrolet was sitting there. It's like my cash machine, I grinned to myself.

I climbed into the back-seat.

Nikki turned to face me.

"In all my time with the Bureau, this is the highest one-off payment I have ever made to an informant," she said.

"We had to hustle to get it," Warren said.

I could not help but glance at the brown envelope. It seemed to be bulging.

"This is $30,000," said Nikki, pulling the bills with their unique dry papery scent out of the envelope.

The counting and signing ritual followed.

"Remember," Nikki said, "you are Morrison."

She smiled with an empathy I'd never seen before.

"We will be in touch next week," she said as I stepped out.

I could not wait to tell Munique. She had to be confident that I'd not lost my mind. She had trusted me to make this leap into the unknown. The least I could do was put a roof over her head.

I was anxious to begin to show my worth too. And so when an email arrived the following week from a Canadian aviation broker, I said quietly to myself: "Yesssssssss."

'Larry' had a lot of Iranian clients, and one was in a heap of trouble: my old nemesis, Alireza Valadkhani.

Valadkhani has been arrested in Spain. Can you help? Larry

I needed more information, and drafted several replies before settling on phraseology that was non-committal.

Just got your email. So he was arrested huh? For what?

The chain continued.

Apparently, he was trying to re-export those ex-Israeli Defense Force Bell 212s to Iran through a Spanish businessman. His colleagues in Iran contacted me late last night to see if I can help.

I wasn't altogether surprised. Valadkhani's was the first name I'd spilled to my inquisitors in Cape Town, and the CIA had been watching his movements. He'd continued to pursue the former IDF Bells - the same aircraft Neil and I had inspected in Tel Aviv!

But the US State Department had been watching the much-travelled Bells since at least 2008, when three of them were temporarily housed in Sweden. The US Embassy in Stockholm had pressed the Swedes - successfully – to postpone their re-export to Spain until certain equipment could be removed.

Eventually – in May 2009 – the three choppers were shipped to Spain. Two Spanish businessmen - Bedia García and Torres Gallego – were the owners but they had signed a part-ownership deal with Valadkhani.

For two years, the CIA worked with their Spanish counterparts to track possible buyers. When I disclosed some of Valadkhani's previous activities, the Americans stepped up their surveillance.

On May 25th 2011 Spanish police swooped on a warehouse in an industrial estate in Navas del Ray, near Madrid. García and Gallego were arrested along with four Iranians, among them Valadkhani.

He had come to Spain to arrange the sale of the helicopters to a company in Barcelona. He had arrived that very morning and headed to the warehouse accompanied by an Iranian lawyer who owned a small aviation business in Barcelona.

I promised Larry I'd reach out to lawyers in Dubai that I knew and had been involved with Valadkhani, who had a front company in the Emirate.

I went through the motions of trying to get Valadkhani freed. I knew he could be a rich and unwitting source of intelligence that Nikki and Warren would relish. But I also knew Valadkhani was a catch who would not be quickly freed. And I knew my information about him had helped focus the Joint Terrorism Task Force on his activities.

For the next two years, Valadkhani was kept under house arrest in Madrid, with no trial date set. His passport was confiscated and he had to post bail of more than $600,000. He was out of the sanctions-busting business and in a weird Iberian limbo.

*

It was the morning of June 22nd, 2011. I was heading out the front door for my morning jog, my normal route down 26th Street and San Vicente, Wilshire and Bundy, near Pinkberry and Whole Foods and ending at the Santa Monica Pier.

I saw a few news trucks zipping past. This being LA, I didn't think anything of it. They make news out of everything and I decided to make a left onto Montana Avenue.

It was a beautiful, sun kissed Southern Californian morning. People were out and about. The Koo-girls with their power walks, the skinny girls with their pedometers, the running and walking clubs with their identical shirts. The dog walkers and the pensioners. All wanting to get their Vitamin D from the SoCal sunshine.

I was averaging a nice pace towards the beach when I saw a bunch of activity at Third Street. Police vehicles, news vans, reporters and the road being blocked off. A hive of activity. I slowed down to gather with the curious crowd. The view down the road showed more police and agents in their FBI raid jackets. Something of interest must be happening I thought. Not wanting to have more lactic acid build up in my legs, I decided to continue my jog.

Once I returned home, I switched on the TV to the morning news show *Good Day LA*. *"Breaking News: Whitey Bulger arrested in Santa Monica."*

The elusive South Boston crime boss, one of the FBI's most wanted men and who eluded them for sixteen years, living just a few blocks from me. A few blocks of physical distance, but, what different worlds we lived in, I thought. Every day when he went out his front door, he must have feared capture by the very people I was sharing intelligence with; and every day as I exited my front door, I was fearing the very end this man ordered for many an associate he worked with.

Trade and financial sanctions have long had a place in international affairs—from the high-profile sanctions applied to South Africa under apartheid to their increasing use as a substitute for military intervention in countries including Iraq, Libya, Iran, Cuba, Sudan and most recently Russia, where they are pending. They've been used to discourage countries from building nuclear weapons, abusing human rights or invading their neighbors. Such sanctions, however, have been controversial because they have appeared to lack the cohesion and determination of allies to make them work effectively.

Banks including HSBC, ABN Amro, Standard Chartered, Lloyds, Barclays, Credit Suisse and BNP-Paribas all have been slapped with multi-billion dollar fines for their involvement in money laundering and tax evasion charges with regards to their Iranian deals.

I was now well into my time as an informant for the FBI's Joint Terrorism Task Force, LA division. The world's eyes were on Iran and news reports every week surfaced about either a bank or a company being fined or charged for trying to circumvent the sanctions against Iran

My meetings with Nikki and Warren had a wide variety of venues: public parks, parked cars, Starbucks and Embassy Suites hotels for more involved conversations. I handed over USB drives containing Skype conversations with Iranian clients; we pored over bank transactions.

At the time there was no higher priority for the US than to apply and toughen sanctions against Iran as it showed no willingness to compromise on its nuclear program, and was incidentally stirring sectarian problems in neighboring Iraq.

I enjoyed the work and felt I was doing something useful. I was no scholar of international diplomacy or geopolitics, but didn't need much expertise to conclude that a nuclear-armed Iran would be a bad thing.

But the work was also taxing, and being a confidential informant inevitably allows a certain level of paranoia to seep into your brain. And it wasn't just Iran: there were a lot of plates to spin.

Luke Miller was one of them.

CHAPTER THIRTEEN

LOSING MY SMUGGLEGINITY
September 2011

C hloe arrived on a bright September morning in 2011, my first born. Like every father I remember the exact moment with utter clarity: the intense emotions of euphoria, protectiveness and no little apprehension all colliding with the piercing cries of a newborn child.

Munique had been admitted to the Beverly Hills hospital the day before, impatient after more than nine months for the moment to arrive.

As I held Chloe for the first time and stared into her eyes, I was overwhelmed, as if I didn't deserve her or was woefully ill-equipped to protect and raise her. The evidence was soon to arrive, thankfully as comedy. The pediatrician wafted in to check on my daughter and then as she left, said casually: "You need to change her diaper."

Me. Baby. Diaper. It might as well have been an origami challenge.

My daughter seemed to be looking at me as I changed her, though of course her vision was far from defined. Two big brown eyes fixed on me, testing my ability. Two little feet kicking in the air. Amid all the challenges I faced, all the pressure from my US colleagues to be a valued confidential source, there was something inexplicably comforting about being alone with this extraordinary creation. This little person would be with me until the day I left this world.

The last few weeks of Munique's pregnancy had been fraught. Four months after arriving in Los Angeles there had been no progress on my requests in return for the flow of intelligence I was providing. I needed an immunity agreement, visa assistance for Munique to gain health insurance and relocation expenses. But the wheels of the federal bureaucracy were turning exceptionally slowly. I felt like I was on the back-burner – and much worse liable to prosecution as party to some of the illicit deals that were being made.

Munique's temporary six-month visa made her ineligible for medical insurance, so I would have to pay the full cost of her giving birth in a Los Angeles hospital. And I was still out-of-pocket on the substantial sums I had spent relocating.

With Munique about to give birth, I wrote a long email to a trusted government contact.

"This has been the worse state I have been financially and emotionally in my life and all because I thought I made the right decision," I confided to her.

I also raised a warning flag. "Really sensitive info is being passed to me but there is nothing in it for me anymore to pass on this info or to continue keeping my "clients" in contact with me."

Like Mr Luke Miller.

Within a sleepless week of Chloe's arrival, he was back in touch.

"Congratulations on your newborn."

"Mr Miller," I said with ill-disguised impatience, "how can

I be of service?"

"I need to move 108 pallets of cigarettes from the UAE to Riga, Latvia."

He was never one for conventional requests.

"It needs to happen next week. Customs are secured at that end and the shipment must be marked on the airway bill as textiles. Can you do this?"

Cigarette smuggling. It may sound prosaic, when compared to cocaine, missiles and aircraft. But it's lucrative. Criminal organizations, terror groups, corrupt officials – they all know they can make serious money from mankind's addiction to tobacco.

I wanted to sound a little detached to Miller after all the fuss about the Ivorian deal that was never concluded.

"Are you sure this will happen?" I asked.

"Barry, I'm paying the plane myself. This is my cigarettes. It will happen. You will get paid, tell me your fee. Can you get me a plane or not?"

He sounded impatient and he did not like to be doubted.

"Sure. Tell me the quantity and how will it be packaged. What brand of cigarettes? Who will be the shipper and consignee?"

"I will email you all the details."

And he did: 108 pallets of M1 cigarettes packaged in L&M sleeves. This meant that very generic cigarettes, commonly known as cheap whites, were being packaged as a premium brand. Miller's client was Raitis Kosnovs, a smuggling baron in Latvia and a man known to punish those who did not meet his expectations.

If there was one thing I was really good at it was finding planes. I'd had nearly a decade of scouring the aviation market for this or that.

Within 24 hours I had found an IL-76 and began making arrangements for the flight, from Fujairah International Airport.

This time, Miller walked the walk. He paid $90,000 in cash to the flight operator and delivered the pallets to the cargo warehouse for palletizing. He also arranged two sets of documents for the aircraft. One showed cigarettes as the export; the other showed textiles as the import. The crew would carry these documents with them, fully aware of the scam. They didn't care so long as they got paid.

On October 10th, 2011 flight number AZS 4004 departed for Riga, carrying 'textiles.' But something went wrong.

As I tiptoed downstairs the following morning, careful not to wake a sleeping child and her sleeping mother, I noticed that Miller had called me five times overnight.

I called him immediately.

"So, the crew submitted the wrong paperwork," he said, raising his voice. I should have made coffee before the call.

"Now I have to pay duty on all those cigarettes! It defeats the purpose!"

He was trying to blame me for hiring incompetents. Miller liked to do that. The truth was rather different. When offloading one of the pallets, a forklift truck had accidentally torn one of the boxes. Packets of cigarettes cascaded onto the tarmac. Kosnovs had to pay an additional $20,000 in bribes to get the cigarettes released as 'textiles.'

I wasn't about to take the blame for the sort of random incident that can wreck any smuggling operation. When Miller calmed down, he accepted that I had fulfilled my role. Whether Kosnovs had leant on him for the additional $20,000 I didn't wish to know.

I had issues to deal with at home, anyway. Neither Munique nor I had been able to adapt to life in L.A. The US west coast might have a similar climate to Cape Town, bit there the similarities ended. Our neighborhood was quiet, and parents followed a rigorous routine of delivering children to school, rushing to work via the Starbucks drive-in and quiet evenings behind the walls of their suburban mock-mansions. There were few opportunities to meet people, and our freedom of action was limited by a demanding baby. I was also beginning to lose faith in the US government's desire to provide me with the assistance necessary to stay.

So at the end of 2011, we packed everything up again, including the four dogs – who seemed equally unsettled – and booked our return passage. It seemed the right thing to do, but would only land me in greater trouble.

My handlers were sorry to see us go, but more than ready to keep the relationship alive. They didn't have too many assets with the range of illicit contacts I possessed, including the irrepressible Luke Miller.

*

On a sweltering morning early in 2012, I stood in the international departures hall at Dubai airport, watching this global hub in full swing as it dispatched humanity to every corner of the globe. I was waiting for my first face-to-face encounter with Luke Miller, to plan a massive cigarette smuggling enterprise. Except that I had made both the US federal government and Belgian intelligence aware of the plot.

I had arranged transport for the smuggling stint with the same company that had made the flight to Latvia. But this time, we needed a Boeing 747. Miller paid $200,000 for a plane based at Ras al-Khaimah Airport in Dubai to fly to Liège in Belgium, laden with 25 million cigarettes.

Miller arranged for textiles and computer scrap parts to be mixed among the boxes of cigarettes.

My contact in Belgian intelligence, Nicholas, was very much looking forward to the plane's arrival.

I was apprehensive about meeting Miller. Some of these bigtime smugglers had succeeded precisely because they were so good at reading people, at detecting disloyalty or betrayal.

And then he came into view, striding confidently along the concourse. I knew instantly among the dozens of people milling through the terminal that this was my man – a tall, muscular figure in a loose white V-neck shirt, tailored jeans and dark sunglasses. You could smell the money.

It helped that walking a respectful half-pace behind was a 300-pound, six-foot-six African American, carrying Miller's bag.

"Barry! Nice to meet you after all this time," said Miller with a gleaming grin. His enormous hand swallowed mine in a handshake.

"This is Big Mike," he continued, gesturing to his impassive follower. "He'll help us with, you know, security."

"Big Mike, right," I said.

He just glared at me.

One of Miller's four burner phones rang. After a conversation lasting less than 30 seconds, he hung up and dropped the phone into a garbage can.

The first thing he did when we arrived in Paris was to buy two more phones. He must be keeping the handset-makers in business, I thought.

We checked into his favorite hotel near the Place Vendome before a late dinner. Miller began to relax over a bottle of Bordeaux. Perhaps he had decided to trust me, or perhaps he wanted to lull me into a false sense of security.

He had a lugubrious side, dwelling on the unfortunate deaths of so many friends and associates. One had been shot in Cambodia; his girlfriend had suffered an embolism and died in front of him while they were on holiday in Thailand. Maybe I should be sparing about my time in Mr Miller's company, I thought.

*

The railway terminus in Liège is an architectural triumph, a concoction of steel, glass and white concrete melded into organic shapes geometrical patterns. It was a bold statement by a city synonymous with industrial decline, much in evidence as we travelled to its airport on the outskirts.

Liège-Bierset is predominantly a cargo hub, a collection of warehouses around a single runway.

Miller said he needed to see the client who was buying the cigarettes, all 25 million of them, and I used his absence to contact Nicholas.

We met in the virtually deserted terminal building. Liège

was no holiday destination. He was sitting with a colleague.

"Hello Barry - you look young for such a dangerous job," he said with a mischievous smirk.

"We have three teams ready for the job," he said. "We will post a reconnaissance team at the warehouse. Then we will have one team at each entry/exit point of the airport. Once the trucks are loaded, we will follow them to the warehouse where they are supposed to offload. Then we will move in with our teams and the Federal Police for the seizure."

The plane was not due until after midnight and Miller wanted me to supervise the offloading onto trucks. It was going to be a long, tense night.

Nicholas had some cheering words for me as we parted.

"You know you are doing a very dangerous job. These people will kill you if they know you set them up. Be careful."

Despite his flamboyant use of phones, Miller was not very consistent about security. Later that evening, at the Swissport warehouse, he made the apparently basic error of showing his real passport to the security manager, who scanned it.

He checked arrangements inside the warehouse and seemed confident nothing could go wrong. As we stepped outside, he pointed to several trucks with Irish plates.

"Ours," he said, with a self-satisfied look.

"I'm going back to the hotel. Let me know when the aircraft arrives and the trucks are being loaded."

"And Barry – don't disappoint me."

It was a sneak preview of the real Luke Miller. I thought I was in Liège, not *In Bruges*.

*

Arretez! Arretez!

I put my head down and ran.

It was 4:30am, and everything was going wrong. The local police had decided to raid the airport warehouse. The three trucks had been impounded; their drivers arrested.

I had to get Miller out of the hotel before his client made sure he never left it alive. Belgian intelligence believed it was the terrorist splinter group Real IRA.

I dialed his room.

"We need to get out. Now! The police are at the warehouse. I'll meet you downstairs."

Within half-an-hour we were boarding the first train of the day for Paris. Miller was apoplectic.

It turned out that two of the trucks had headed not for the warehouse near Liège but straight for the Dutch border. Belgian intelligence had not notified their Dutch colleagues, and the police had decided to raid the airport before the last truck could leave. Nor did they have any idea I was working for Belgian intelligence. They might even have shot me.

It was an example of the dysfunctionality of the Belgian security services that would later be exploited by Islamist extremist's intent on attacking Europe.

As for Miller, he had already been paid – and just wanted out of Belgium as fast as possible, before the Belgian authorities or his Irish clients could apprehend him.

He vanished as soon as we reached Paris. I wearily made my way to Charles de Gaulle airport for the long haul home, only to be astonished when he contacted me just weeks later for another tilt at the European appetite for knocked-off smokes.

Her Majesty's Revenue and Customs had learned of the

Liège fiasco through intelligence channels – and their interest was piqued by the Irish connection. Smuggling and terrorism all wrapped up in one case: they were very interested to meet me, even more so when I told them that Miller was planning an encore, with the curtain being raised once more in Dubai.

And so I found myself back in the Emirate in the spring of 2012, sitting in a fish restaurant with Paul and Lara. They were from the investigative branch of the UK Customs agency. Both were seasoned investigators in their mid-forties.

Lara had green eyes and a plain brown bob and dressed soberly without adornments.

"Seems like you've been keeping busy with some interesting people," she said as we settled in.

I told them of the Liège operation, and they made feverish notes.

"The next shipment is 28 million cigarettes, which they want delivered in Luxembourg as they don't want to risk Liège again. The brand will be Palace," I said, a cigarette that had actually been discontinued by its makers, JTI.

In reality the cigarettes would be from the cheapest tobacco offloaded by Chinese manufacturers and mixed with anything from wood-shavings to hay.

"I'm meeting Miller this evening," I said.

They looked at me with bemusement. How did this young South African dealer in helicopter parts end up as Luke Miller's partner in a massive cigarettes racket?

The Address Montgomerie Golf Club nestles among expensive villas and artificial lakes in the richest part of a very rich place. Having just returned from L.A., it immediately reminded me of Beverly Hills.

This was the place Miller called home.

At midnight – after I had waited two hours – the unmistakable purr of a Ferrari 458 alerted his arrival. He was wearing his trademark white V-neck shirt, no doubt to show off the work he'd been doing in the gym.

"Everything is confirmed - plane will leave as discussed and we have customs organized on the other end," I promised. It was true customs were organized; just not in the way he thought.

"I need to pay for the plane and they will only pay me after we deliver. So this is all on me," Miller said, fixing me with a glare.

A few weeks later, the plane carrying more than 28 million cigarettes touched down in Luxembourg, to be greeted by customs agents and a sizeable police presence. It was the biggest ever airfreight haul of counterfeit cigarettes in Europe.

The British were delighted to have been at the heart of such a major bust, which was worth at least 10 million dollars in lost excise revenue.

Lara invited me to London to be debriefed and presented me with an envelope containing nearly $40,000, an extraordinary reward by the standards of the British government.

CHAPTER FOURTEEN

ENEMY OF THE STATE

March 2012

N*othing for Mahala: Inside SA's Illegal Helicopter Activities.*
The Spy That Came in from the Cold.
Two headlines in the Sunday Times, South Africa's
leading weekend newspaper.

It was March 11, 2012. I had been born into a hurricane,
and was about to be swept up in another one. The story of the
lunch at Ten Bompas was out.

Subpoenas followed; it was a traumatic time for both myself
and Munique. I retained a lawyer but for several months we
had little contact with the prosecuting authorities. It seemed
the story might even die away, I thought – and hoped.

My hope was abruptly shattered on September 22nd 2012,
as Munique and I were about to check in at Cape Town airport
for a flight to Dubai.

I had a follow-up meeting scheduled with UK Customs.

"Are you Mr. Barend Hendrik Oberholzer?"

It was a question dressed as an accusation.

"I am Brigadier Olivier from the Directorate of Special
Investigations. I am placing you under arrest."

Brigadier Oliver was flanked by two other officers. One
was Colonel Adrian Schilz and the other, also a Colonel, went
unnamed.

Munique began to cry, to the apparent pleasure of the officers. To add to the humiliation, they handcuffed me in the presence of hundreds of travelers, led me from the airport building and took me to Durbanville police station, some 25km away.

The charge was a crudely ingenious attempt to revive an old business dispute that had long been withdrawn. The purpose was revenge for the embarrassment I had caused the Deputy President of South Africa and Mama Gugu. The timing was also perfectly planned, arrested on a Thursday afternoon on the eve of a banking holiday weekend, the officers knowing full well that it won't be until the Tuesday before I can be brought before a magistrate.

Why otherwise would a specialized crimes unit be involved in such a petty non-issue? Why would the Brigadier transport me to the police station in his personal car, and make several calls along the way, including one to a General, confirming my arrest?

And then there was the questioning.

"So, you worked for the Americans?" the unnamed Colonel asked.

I didn't answer.

As I was waiting to be fingerprinted, to have my picture taken and officially processed, a policeman asked the Brigadier: "I didn't know you were still working dockets and doing arrests?"

"Only on high-profile cases," he responded.

It would be several days before I could get a bail hearing, no accident in itself. In the meantime, I would have to share a holding cell with twenty other men. A smell of urine mixed with disinfectant hung in the air. Stinking blankets sat in the corner on top of a few plastic mats.

It was gloomy and cold. I sat with a blanket wrapped around my shoulders, worried sick about Munique and shame my family would feel when they heard about my arrest.

I had to switch to survival mode. I had to adapt.

"How do I become the alpha male in this place?" I asked myself.

Cigarettes.

When my brother brought me a change of clothes, I whispered through the bars.

"Get me as many packs of cigarettes you can. Bring me a jacket and line the pockets with loose cigarettes."

On his next visit I received a jacket lined with ninety loose cigarettes. Luke Miller would be proud, I thought.

As soon as the other detainees saw my loot, they were like vultures. Personalities changed instantly. Each inmate was now my best friend.

"You know your arrest is all over the news," my brother told me.

How curious. Why would the arrest of a businessman for an alleged bad business deal be of national significance?

Someone was feeding the media. Someone who wanted to discredit me, and tarnish my name.

And why would bail in such a case be set at R50 000? I did not have that sort of cash on hand.

After five days in that dismal cell, eating virtually nothing and trading cigarettes for security, my court appearance was finally arranged.

Munique's mother was there, with a clean shirt.

She tried to smile, but her red-rimmed eyes told of the trauma the family were enduring.

"It's going to be OK; we arranged some money," she said.

"Let's hope it's enough."

"We love you."

"Oberholzer!" a police officer shouted.

I was marched to the holding cells. A dark underground floor, packed with the weekend's haul of offenders. Each cell held eighty to a hundred detainees.

As I walked, I was shouted and sworn at, even spat upon. A cell door swung open.

A man whose yellowish eyes matched the color of his parchment skin came straight toward me.

"Any cigarettes or things you want to give? You have some nice shoes." he hissed.

"Go buy your own shoes," I replied and continued past him.

Thankfully my stay in the holding cell lasted but minutes. As I arrived in the courtroom, my lawyer, Asghar Mia hurried over to talk. He looked taken aback at my disheveled and no doubt malodorous appearance.

"They agreed not to oppose bail but only on strict bail conditions: paying R50,000 cash, surrendering your passports, and reporting daily to the police station. Your family arranged the cash so, if you agree, you can be out of here in an hour."

Despite the massive bail amount, I had no choice. And I was bent on revenge.

Brigadier Oliver and Colonel Schilz had requested the

archived docket from the commercial dispute, even though the complaint had been withdrawn. I filed suit for wrongful arrest. It would be the beginning of a long and debilitating war of attrition.

The bail conditions disrupted my intelligence work. Unable to travel, I was of less use to my friends at UK Customs, and my value to various US agencies was also diminished. But my previous information was beginning to bear fruit, or at least advance ongoing investigations.

By the spring of 2013, it was all about cocaine.

CHAPTER FIFTEEN

NOSE CANDY
2013

I needed a partner, someone I and my 'customers' could trust, who could stay cool under pressure, keep his story straight, and who was not confined by trumped-up charges to South Africa.

My brother Marcel was just that partner: mentally tough, discreet, level-headed. And he was able to travel abroad, which was just as well – as keeping up with Luke Miller demanded a thick passport.

Miller's wealth puzzled me. His every venture seemed poorly planned; he had no competent associates; he was rash and temperamental. And he had made plenty of enemies. He lurched from one abortive operation to the next – but apparently untouchable.

In part that was because various US agencies, as well as their counterparts in Britain, had no interest in apprehending Miller. The reason was simple: he led us to all sorts of more dangerous characters, unwittingly sowing a trail of breadcrumbs. Not just in Europe but by 2013 among some powerful organizations in Latin America.

His plan was elaborate to the point of convoluted. He would charter an aircraft in Europe on behalf of his customers and export drilling equipment to a front company in Colombia.

Also among the cargo: industrial batteries.

Those batteries would not stay in Colombia. Instead they would be stuffed with cocaine and re-exported to South Africa. And from there it would be distributed to Europe. The premise was that South African exports were much less likely to be suspected of hiding cocaine.

None of Miller's clients was dull. And the man running the Colombian connection was a British citizen of Pakistani origin known to Miller as 'Burj Boy.'

Burj Boy's real name was Malik. He had left the UK in a hurry as he was being pursued for a massive tax fraud. He'd taken up residence at the extravagant Burj Al-Arab hotel in Dubai (hence the alliterative nickname.)

Shortly before the flight was due to arrive in Colombia, I contacted a special agent at the Department of Homeland Security. They were interested, of course, "in keeping this stuff off the streets." But they were also cautious about working with me and could not make any promises about a reward for information.

"We would require some good faith information on your part, more directly," the Special Agent wrote to me. "We need to get a successful seizure in order to establish your track record. We can possibly provide a small remuneration for a successful seizure, but we would need to establish a relationship after that."

I wasn't overwhelmed by his enthusiasm, but persisted with my efforts to have the shipment intercepted.

The hub for this racket would be a small town on the Colombian-Venezuelan border.

Cucuta is about as different from Dubai as cocaine is from flour. As poor and rutted as the Emirate is rich and polished, it was bathed in humidity and surrounded by slums. Law enforcement had been bought off or intimidated by cartels such as Los Urabenos; vigilantes known as *moscas* kept order in the poor parts of town, which was most of it.

But Cucuta and Dubai had one similarity: they were havens for smugglers and men wanted elsewhere. In Cucuta's case these included El Pulpo, a former car thief who had made himself fabulously rich through shipping cocaine by sea and air to the developed world.

Burj Boy was well-educated and quick on his feet. He also had a raw courage that bordered on the foolhardy. He needed it for this venture: going into business with Los Urabenos was like sharing a home with black mambas.

But he was stunningly indiscreet and made the mistake of not doing due diligence on Luke Miller and his mixed business record. He hired him to organize the logistics, and yet again Miller came to me – even though every operation in which I had been involved had ended badly, and even though I had a few legal issues of my own.

Burj Boy had come to South Africa to check my credentials and character. We had dined at an overpriced restaurant that had spent more money on polished metal fittings than hiring a decent chef.

"The economics of cocaine smuggling is pretty simple," Burj Boy explained.

"My guys will buy a kilo of cocaine in the highlands of Colombia for around $2,000, then watch it accrue value as it makes its way to market. That kilo fetches more than $10,000 by the time I buy it from them. If you get it then to the United States or UK it could sell wholesale for up to $50,000. Break it down into grams to distribute retail, and that same kilo sells for upward of $100,000--more than its weight in gold."

There are 1,000 kilograms in every tonne, and as much as 300 tonnes were leaving Cucuta annually. The margins were good.

My US handlers very much wanted Burj Boy's racket disrupted, but had limited ability to intervene themselves. They were, however, prepared to mediate with South Africa's Organized Crime Unit, which didn't have a very high opinion of me at the time.

Two Homeland Security agents from the embassy in Pretoria accompanied me to a meeting with a former Deputy Police Commissioner, Ganief Daniels.

Daniels, a 30-year veteran of the South African Police Service, was incidentally also my neighbor. His valuable contacts inside the police force as well as in the Cape Town underworld catapulted him to building a wealthy nest egg, something a police pension would not even get close to.

Colonel Roussouw, as head of the Directorate of Priority Crimes (HAWKS) Narcotics Unit, was also present.

I outlined enough of Burj Boy's plan to spark Rossouw's interest.

"I can share much more with you, and I don't want to get paid. I just want my passports back."

"We will certainly see what we can do to assist you," the Colonel said, with what seemed a rather pretentious use of the royal 'we.'

Within a few days, the Hawks, as the squad was known, were back in touch. I explained that I had to recommend a landing strip somewhere in South Africa for Burj Boy's plane.

"Alexander Bay," suggested one officer with a jaw as square as a cartoon character.

Alexander Bay was a small town on the west coast that made its living by diamonds. It had an airstrip that could accommodate the plane I was recommending to Miller. The Hawks would be able to monitor the delivery and follow it to the warehouse where it would be broken up for distribution.

Despite the opportunity to make one of the biggest drugs busts in South African history, Rossouw's former colleagues ultimately declined my offer.

"Those guys at the Commercial Crimes Unit really have the knife in for you. What did you do to piss them off?" Colonel Rossouw asked. Perhaps he never read the papers.

It was something of a relief when Burj Boy abruptly decided to change the routing of his precious cargo to Cotonou in Benin. West Africa had become the favoured conduit for Colombian cartels. States were weak, officials pliable. In recent years, extravagant villas surrounded by tall walls had popped up amid the abject poverty and ramshackle shanties of towns along the coast. Expensive Mercedes weaved among the potholes and carts. Places like Benin and Guinea Bissau were becoming unlikely holiday homes for rich Colombians.

Now that the South African option was no longer in play, the Homeland Security team had decided to intercept the shipment in Cucuta, a highly risky tactic in a town that was a byword for gangsterism.

Despite a mild heart attack, Miller was still involved almost hourly in the operation. It was just too big a payday to surrender, even while hooked up to monitors in an incentive care unit.

"It's time to bring the plane in," he said in a hoarse whisper from his hospital bed.

It wasn't easy to source a plane for a destination like Cucuta. The first question, even from people who didn't ask many questions, was 'Why?' The second was about payment and the third about whether I was out of my mind if I thought they'd wait until reaching Cucuta before getting compensated.

Eventually, several months after the plan was first mooted, someone desperate enough agreed. They had a Ukrainian-registered aircraft in the Netherlands that would fly via Iceland, Canada and Bermuda, carefully avoiding the US.

The venerable Antonov AN12 began its long trek westwards just as the Homeland Security stepped up surveillance in Cucuta. It was October 24th 2013.

Trouble was that a different intelligence stream had led a Colombian anti-narcotics team to the same place at the same time. The following day I received a curt email from my contact at DHS in Washington, exasperated by the expense and risk of keeping a team in Cucuta.

"Same information was also provided to French customs who passed it to the Colombian anti-narcotics unit. That made things a little sticky when they moved in. All warehouses were searched twice with dogs. Negative results."

Unfortunately, this was none too rare in the struggle against the cartels. Intelligence agencies co-operated on an ad hoc basis and jealously guarded their confidential informants.

So on that stifling October afternoon, a DHS team was watching the hangars at Cucuta's airport just as a Colombian unit was sweeping through the gates to search warehouses.

My DHS contact was soon on the phone.

"Who the hell told the Colombians about this? No wonder there was nothing--the Colombians probably tipped off the cartel."

Not a single ounce of cocaine was found that afternoon. When news of the raid reached Miller, he called me.

"Call off the plane," he breathed. "It's not happening. Cucuta's hotter than a poker."

"The plane's half way across the Atlantic," I protested. "Who's going to foot this bill? If I cancel now I will be liable for the full charter fees!"

"Everyone loses, Barry," came the hoarse response. "We couldn't move the stock either. Someone tipped off the local police. It was like a war zone at the airport."

The next call I made was one of the most difficult of my career. The Ukrainian broker yelled so loudly that I would have probably heard him without a phone.

His command of English expletives was impressive.

"You pay! You pay! Full bill you pay!" he shouted.

And so I inherited a debt of $400,000. And the Ukrainian mafia tended to settle disputes with cleavers. I just had to hope they had no affiliates in South Africa; to this day I expect someone called Yuri, with gold teeth and biceps like tree limbs, to knock at my door.

CHAPTER SIXTEEN

BROWN SUGAR
March 2013

"We're at the shopping mall parking lot. I'm waiting for the driver to arrive."

Fat Waz was a caricature of a London gangster. His real name was Wassim and he could have easily been cast in a Guy Ritchie movie. He was bald, overweight, with tattoos on his forearms and an upper lip that curled in contempt every time he spoke. He was a business associate, to use a euphemism, of Burj Boy, who still thought South Africa was a promising entrepot for his products.

Some of their cocaine would be sold in South Africa; the rest would be shipped to the UK and Australia.

Except that this time – on a broiling March day in 2013 – Burj Boy was dealing in brown sugar, not white powder. The brown sugar was impure heroin, which is easier to make than white heroin and can be smoked. There was a thriving market in Europe for it.

Both Burj Boy and Fat Waz were of Pakistani origin, which helped them source the heroin from the wild territories either side of the Pakistan-Afghan border. Wassim's home-town was in Punjab province, half-way between Islamabad and Lahore.

Manufacturers – often linked to or taxed by the Taliban – would buy the raw opium paste from poppy farmers and turn it into heroin. Burj Boy's associates in the sprawling port city of Karachi – some of them family – would then buy the heroin and hide it among anything from rice sacks to soccer balls.

They also had associates in South Africa and Pakistan acquiring weapons on their behalf. One of them was a scrap metal dealer in Johannesburg whose father was a retired brigadier in the Pakistani armored corps. A serving Major General was also an intermediary in the shipping of the 'brown sugar'. No wonder the Pakistani military was compromised when it came to the Taliban and Afghanistan.

The containers would usually be sent from Karachi to Mozambique, where the heroin had less chance of being discovered, before being transported overland to South Africa. It really wasn't difficult.

Some of the heroin would be sold on local markets; most would get repackaged and shipped to Europe.

Fat Waz was Burj Boy's point man in South Africa. Burj Boy preferred to stay in Dubai, keeping a low profile and staying beyond the reach of the British tax authorities.

They communicated on encrypted BlackBerrys which they ordered from a contact in Canada. These were the days before the encrypted applications era like Telegram, Silent Circle and Threema. Fat Waz brandished one of the devices in my face one day.

"Even MI6 and the CIA can't read this," he boasted in his east London accent.

My brother and I were waiting to receive their largest-yet shipment of brown sugar at an empty warehouse not far from the shopping mall. In front of us was a 40-foot shipping container, filled with pallets loaded with wine.

The wine would be supplemented with 130 pounds of brown sugar, loaded under my supervision. Then the container would be loaded onto a freighter for Malta, and broken up for onward shipment to the UK. Its estimated street value was about $2.6 million.

Twenty minutes later, Fat Waz arrived with the goods. I wound up the manual roller-door of the warehouse as the sweat dripped from my forehead. Fat Waz's rental Toyota was followed by a Volkswagen pick-up truck.

A short man in his mid-forties jumped from the truck. He had the complexion of an Indian and the frown of someone who is constantly doing others' dirty work. He walked quickly to the back of the truck and opened the tailgate, and then began unscrewing its panels.

A cocktail of toxic odors wafted from the truck, like a foul stew of burnt ash and swimming pool cleaner. The short Indian began taking out vacuum-packed 'bricks.' There were sixty of them, and each had a stamp.

"What does the stamp mean?" I asked Fat Waz.

"That, my friend, is the stamp of the tribe in Afghanistan that processed the heroin. Each producer adds their stamp. It's like a guarantee of quality," he said with a smirk.

The driver departed with a fistful of cash, and Fat Waz set about concealing the bricks at the bottom of each pallet. He was soon drenched in sweat as he squeezed his flab between the pallets in the oven of the container.

My brother and I watched, careful not to leave our

fingerprints on any of the bricks.

After half-an-hour of hard labor, Fat Waz emerged from the container damp and dirty. But he was satisfied.

"Just to confirm," he said, "container is collected tomorrow and delivered to port, then loaded the following day."

I nodded. I would let him know it was on its way, just as I would let various intelligence agencies know.

*

About a week after the entire consignment was seized in Malta, I received a text message.

My name is Donovan. I have been asked by Malik to arrange your assassination. Can we meet?

Malik was Burj Boy's real name, and he was very upset. Not only had the Colombian operation gone wrong, but now nearly $3 million of his brown sugar was in the hands of the authorities.

I read the text again, searching in vain for an exclamation mark or something to suggest this was a sick joke, or at least a lame attempt at extortion.

It wasn't. It quickly became apparent that Burj Boy had approached Donovan to have me liquidated. But he'd insisted that he would only pay when the job was done. Donovan had demurred, but Burj Boy persisted. Could he get some weapons – untraceable – for a group of Pakistanis that Burj Boy had hired to do the job?

Donovan by now had tired of Burj Boy's antics, and sent me the text. He might move in underground circles but – as I was soon to find out – he was also a confidential informant for the South African police. He wanted to warn me that a bunch of psychopathic Pakistanis, including Fat Waz's cousin, could be on my trail. He wasn't wrong.

That same day, six south Asians arrived at my previous offices, where I had met Fat Waz a couple of times. They had asked several people where I might be found. Luckily none of them knew, or if they did weren't saying. They probably saved my life.

I needed to know more, and reached out to Donovan. If these would-be assassins were even half-competent, they would soon track me down.

I texted Donovan to meet me at a coffee shop in a Cape Town suburb – somewhere suitably public. When he arrived, I watched him from across the street, making sure he was not with anyone. Then I texted him, telling him that I would only meet him at the police station nearby.

To my astonishment, he agreed. That's when I discovered his work as a police informant.

"Fat Waz is determined to rub you out," he said with a look of pity.

He explained that Fat Waz was embarrassed that he had entrusted me with so much information. He felt he had to regain his reputation in the syndicate. And his cousin, Ullah Khan, had been entrusted with the job.

"I meet a lot of unsavory characters," Donovan said. "But Ullah Khan is among the worst. Each letter of his name is tattooed on his fingers. He has the yellowest eyes I have ever seen; he looks like a poisonous snake."

It wasn't a comforting meeting. The police promised they would try to find him, but they didn't seem eager to come to my aid. I wondered why not.

One evening, a short time later, I received a text from Marcel.

"At John Dory's. Pakistanis have cornered me."

I am not easily frightened, but at that moment I was petrified. A cold sweat enveloped me.

John Dory's was a local seafood restaurant. I jumped into my car and raced there.

In desperation I called Colonel Rossouw, who had handled surveillance of meetings I had had with Fat Waz.

"Under no circumstances enter the restaurant, Barry. Wait till our ground units arrive. I will be there in 15 minutes."

When I arrived at John Dory's, I sat outside in my car for five minutes, trying to get a sight of what was going on inside. I recognized my brother from the back of his head. Opposite him at a table were Fat Waz, a man I took to be Ullah Khan and another Pakistani. He had just stepped out to get take-out when he was cornered by the three men.

My phone buzzed. Another text from Marcel.

Bad guys with me at John Dory's. They want to see you. Now.

"Shit!" I said under my breath. There was no sign of the police. I had no choice and climbed out of the car. After taking several deep breaths, I entered the restaurant.

The look of triumph on Fat Waz's face induced a wave of nausea. I imagined a hostage situation ending in a shoot-out. These guys had no idea the police were on their way.

"Are you working with the coppers?" Fat Waz demanded.

He was so furious that veins were pumping in his neck and on his bald head.

"Of course not," I said, with as much incredulity as I could muster. "Who told you that?"

Ullah Khan chimed in.

"OK, you won't mind doing a lie detector test then. You and bro. If the police find out, it will be your last day on earth."

"Not a problem," I said.

Fat Waz got up. I couldn't tell whether he was armed, and at that moment I very much did not want the police charging in. He gave me the name of an Irish pub in what might be called the 'cheating side' of town.

"One o'clock. Don't try anything stupid."

Minutes after they had driven off, Colonel Rossouw called me. He was waiting at a nearby gas station and badly needed to meet me.

He was very unhappy.

"Why did you go into the restaurant? I told you not to. You could have been killed. Now they're gone; we can't do anything."

For some reason, I decided not to tell him about the imminent lie-detector test. My instinct told me that Marcel and I had to resolve this crisis. I didn't trust the police not to make the situation worse. And even if Fat Waz and his odious cousin were arrested, how many more of the Pakistani mafia were out there? They had already found Marcel, who had a teenage son and baby daughter, and might yet find Munique and Chloe.

*

"Are you a snitch?"

Marcel and I were in the backroom of a dingy Irish pub, with the body odor of three large Pakistanis and the smell of stale beer for company.

The "enforcer" spat the question out, enunciating each word slowly – his discolored teeth on show like venomous fangs. He was a well-known figure in Cape Town's underworld, a man with biceps the size of most men's thighs, a carefully trimmed beard and an outcrop of hair defying the race to baldness. I'm not disclosing his real name for my own safety and that of my family.

He had already beaten Marcel with a quick back hand slap and appeared to have enjoyed it. There was no escape; there were five of them and the door was locked. We had to convince them we were 'clean.'

He leant forward – his bad breath hitting my face in waves. The tiny chair he was sitting on creaked in pain as it supported his 300-pound frame. A gun, with the safety catch off, sat on the table as further intimidation.

"You're working for the Hawks, aren't you? Maybe the CIA too? We know you have an American passport."

That alarmed me; they knew more than I anticipated. Did they know I was the informant in the Iranian helicopter deal that had got the Vice President into hot water? I had never been named publicly, but there had been enough details in the press coverage to implicate me.

"Are we your playmates?" he said, tilting his head to one side and flashing a menacing half-smile.

"No." I tried to sound indignant. "I've never worked for the police. And nor has Marcel."

I looked at my brother. His cheek was covered in blood; I could even smell the sickly iron. He looked vacant, frozen.

I knew that one crack in our cover story – one misstep – and our bodies would end up in a garbage tip or as food for the sharks in the bay.

A lie detector was strapped to Marcel's blood-stained arm.

"No," he said with surprising force when asked for the second or third time whether he was working for the CIA.

His eyes were fixed defiantly on his interrogator.

As the polygraph machine registered its first results, I told myself to resist any rash, instinctive act of resistance, to relax my body and stay loose. Plan, focus, banish fear.

There was – of all things – an adult magazine on the table in front of the enforcer. I imagined grabbing it and thrusting it into his eyes, grabbing his weapon at the same time.

The questioning went on for an hour. Perhaps their lie detector was not working properly; perhaps they didn't know how to read the results. Or just maybe Marcel and I were better liars than we gave ourselves credit for. Our story remained consistent; we did not flinch. And the fact that we had come for the test willingly and confidently probably impressed our inquisitors.

The enforcer would probably have killed me, but Fat Waz seemed persuaded that they'd over-reacted.

Just as it seemed the interrogation would go on for hours, Fat Waz brought it to a close.

"Enough. You can go. But we're watching you. Someone has been snitching. And we'll find out who."

They never did, probably because they just weren't very smart. Burj Boy died in mysterious circumstances back in Dubai in June 2015. The word was that an Afghan drug trafficker had him murdered over a substantial unpaid debt. He was just 35.

Fat Waz left South Africa for a while as the heat rose, but last I heard he had come back, more persuaded than ever that I was betraying him and Burj Boy.

CHAPTER SEVENTEEN

PRISONOMICS
October 2014

My father's gradual decline into alcoholism and then dementia finally ended on an October day in 2014. I was driving along the on one of the most beautiful stretches of road in the wine country on my way home from a meeting when my brother called.

"Dad just passed away," he said.

Though the crackle of the phone connection was audible, both of us fell silent for at least thirty seconds.

"I'm on my way."

I was flanked by beautiful vineyards on both sides of the road. The sky was cloudless. A baby blue. The surrounding mountains was a darker blue, almost black against the sky. My eyes watered as I realized I will never see my dad again.

During the last month of his life, Dad had called me saying he was hurt. But he sounded drunk again. I carelessly decided to leave him a few hours so he could sober up, thinking he was crying wolf.

When my brother and I finally went to his apartment, we found him slumped against the bed. He had fallen and fractured his shoulder and was in real pain. But his gaze was the opposite of accusatory. His brown, rheumy eyes were beseeching – as if to seek forgiveness for the years of hurt he had caused the family as he slipped from fast-track diplomat to alcoholic recluse.

Alcohol had brought on erratic behavior and slurred speech, even when he wasn't drunk. But once he was in hospital, he inexplicably changed, perhaps instinctively knowing that he had just a few weeks to be reconciled with his family and prepare for the next journey.

He was kinder, gentler – but confused in a way that upset all those who had known his sharp intellect and mental agility.

The day he died, he could scarcely talk. But as we sat around his bed, dreading the inevitable but longing for his suffering to end, he suddenly looked around the room and said as if lucidly:

"Don't sweat the small stuff."

Despite his flaws, I admired him to the end, and his parting left a deep, dark void. I replayed so many memories of the better days, when he would regale us as children with the stories of the places he had been. I could even smell that leather jacket he had favored; I could see him on the touchline at rugby games urging me on. But I also shivered at the more recent memories of a confused, lonely old man looking out of his apartment window. I would often take a long diversion to avoid going past that place.

In reality I think I lost my dad many years before. His mind had gone before his body. There were a lot of bad times but a weird calm relief came over me as I knew he would be free from pain now. In some way I wanted to go with him. How good would it have felt to be in a place with no anger, no resentment, no judgement, no debt. But for now I had to stay behind and fight my battle. He would've wanted me to.

I threw myself into studying and work to occupy my mind, and perhaps to find assurance that I would not let whatever talents I had wither on the vine like he had. It also helped that we were expecting a second daughter; the younger generation brought us joy just as the older brought us grief.

I was doing a correspondence course at the American Military University on counter-intelligence. I found the work fascinating and at the same time shuddered at my naivety just a few years earlier as I had touted for business in Tehran.

On the morning of May 22nd 2015, there was a loud knock at the door.

Through the window I saw Colonel Adrian Schilz, the senior officer from the Hawks who was also present at my initial arrest in September 2012. I was overcome by a debilitating queasiness. Finally, he thought he had enough for another stab at me.

Schilz was short and unkempt, the sort of man who would look a mess in a $1,000 suit. His shirt buttons strained with the effort of holding back his body fat; his face would move through a spectrum of reds as he spoke.

As I opened the door, he barged in as if I was some flight risk or heavily-armed fugitive.

"Barend Oberholzer, you know me, I am Colonel Schilz. This here is Warrant Officer Rudi and that is Warrant Officer Smith. I am placing you under arrest for fraud."

Schilz had clearly rehearsed this visit. He spoke slowly and deliberately as if trying to remember a particularly challenging passage from a Samuel Beckett play. You could look into his eyes and almost see his brain straining with the effort.

The buttons down the front of his shirt strained with his every movement. His face and cheeks would go a deeper crimson with every expression of emotion.

I was his little project. If only he could pin some phony charge on me that long and understandably delayed promotion might finally be his. He had been interviewing associates, painting me as a psychopathic white-collar criminal. He also wanted revenge for the lawsuit I had brought against him and the Minister of Police for wrongful arrest three years earlier.

Munique heard the commotion and came into the hallway. As soon as she saw Schilz, she knew this would not be over quickly.

The other two officers seemed embarrassed by his overbearing attitude and his insistence I be placed in handcuffs. It was as if he was begging me to resist.

As I was led out of the door, I turned to Munique – her eyes now glassy with the first of many tears that would follow. "Don't worry, it's going to be okay, I'll be home soon."

She nodded vaguely, perhaps aware that even I did not believe what I was saying, and kissed me on the forehead wiping away a tear running down her cheek.

Schiltz grinned. It was the closest I came to knocking him down. His self-satisfaction continued at the police station, as he called prosecutors and senior officers.

I reminded him that he had to notify the US Consulate of my arrest, as I was a US citizen.

He had been longing for that moment.

"I have 48 hours to notify the Embassy of an arrest, and I will advise my head office to do so at hour 47."

I was led into a gloomy cell that smelt of disinfectant and excrement. I slumped onto a bench in the corner, thinking about the tears Munique would now be shedding, the questions from Chloe. Why had Daddy not come to pick her up from kindergarten? Why had he gone without saying goodbye? When would he come back?

Adding to my stress, and perhaps feeding off it, my liver began to misbehave. It was a condition I had lived with since infancy – elevated levels of bilirubin that could bring on intense pain suddenly.

A prison doctor saw me briefly, but then I was returned to the holding cell with a fetid blanket and told to 'sleep it off.' I had a court appearance in six hours' time.

I was moved to a court cell soon after daybreak. There was a collection of holding pens in the basement of the Magistrates' building. I was the only white man among dozens of defendants.

The court bailiff called my name and climbed the stairs from that Dantean scene into a brightly lit courtroom. Schilz was there, relishing my discomfort and disorientation. My regular lawyer was overseas and my family had found a substitute at short notice. But he was unprepared and made a feeble case for bail. I felt a noose tightening around my neck.

The prosecutor requested my continued detention for seven days so further investigations could be carried out. My useless lawyer scarcely challenged the request and the magistrate remanded me at the Allandale Correctional Facility.

Allandale – run by gangs, not warders, and fueled by drugs. The prison allocates different gangs into three separate sections. The various gangs are generally called "The Numbers" and they are enormously powerful in their given shared cells.

Established in 1911, the gang is divided into three factions: the 26s, the 27s and the 28s. Each arm of the gang serves a different purpose. The 26s are responsible for getting cash, the 27s are the law-keepers and the 28s are the warriors.

The Numbers Gang is particularly dangerous because of its influence in the prison system and the level of violence the gang demands of their members, being notorious for attacks on prison guards and warders.

As I awaited to be transferred, I was given a slice of stale bread and undrinkable coffee. I gave the bread away to another defendant who beamed as if he'd been invited to dine at a five-star restaurant.

I badly wanted to break down and sob, but such weakness in the presence of hardened criminals and desperate drug addicts would be suicidal. Eventually, seventy of us were frog-marched to a waiting van and crammed inside. The stench was unbearable: stale alcohol, body odor, unwashed feet wafting through the unventilated truck. The detainees shouted obscenities at passers-by on the street; this truly was Bedlam.

I was parched; just one drop of water…. But I was also ashamed. How had I let it come to this? How would my family cope? How would they explain all this to friends?

As soon as I had been fingerprinted and photographed, a warden barked at me.

"Oberholzer!" a warden shouted. "Follow me."

He took me through a maze of steel-barred gates and

concrete lined hallways to A-Section. As I passed through the other sections, the inmates were peering through the bars, shouting at me. I avoided their cruel, lascivious looks, but caught the eye of one inmate.

He was heavy-set, with gangster tattoos and mean amber eyes. He looked at me as if stalking prey. It was Fat Waz's cousin, Ullah Khan.

He'd been arrested and charged with conspiracy to commit murder, as one of the Pakistani gang that had tried to kill me. Despite my encounter with a lie detector and now my presence in prison, both Ullah Khan and Fat Waz still harboured suspicions. Perhaps even the police had told them of my role as an informant. I could put nothing past Schilz.

A sickening claustrophobia overcame me as I realized no guardian angel was about to pluck me from this nightmare, no attorney was about to persuade the magistrate to change his mind. I was in Allandale: the stories about violence, rape, tuberculosis, the psychopaths mixed with the mentally ill, corrupt wardens…all seemed very close at hand.

I was ushered into an office, given a "welcome pack" of a roll of toilet paper, a toothbrush and toothpaste. The warden let me to cell A-3. A non-gang affiliated cell – or so I was led to believe.

As he slammed the steel door behind me, I surveyed some eighty cell-mates. Some were sleeping on the floor, some were playing a board game, others smoked weed, crack or cigarettes.

I made my way to the corner and sat on a plastic bucket when the cell boss, or *huisbaas*, came to me.

Welcome to Cell A-3.

As the *huisbaas* was going through the do's and don'ts of the cell, my mind raced. I had had no sleep; my liver condition was not improving; I could even imagine taking my own life. I feared I would be subjected to what was known as 'the slow puncture' - a gang-orchestrated rape of a prisoner, led by a prisoner known to carry the HIV virus.

Around the time of my detention, a senior judge had condemned the conditions in prison for those awaiting trial, who should be held innocent until proven guilty. He said he was "deeply shocked by the extent of overcrowding, unsanitary conditions, sickness, emaciated physical appearance of detainees and deplorable living conditions."

But the judge's report if anything airbrushed the reality. Drains were blocked so a bucket was used to flush what passed for the toilet – the only one for eighty of us. My newly acquired bunk had no bedding, but what bedding there was crawled with lice. We shared our cell with other creatures too: cockroaches and mosquitoes feeding off the squalor.

And yet there were incredible gestures of solidarity and empathy among this collection of the discarded and unwanted.

"Do you want to phone your family?"

I looked up.

"My name's Jan."

His tired face and sad eyes spoke volumes.

"Yes, please," I said – almost in a whisper.

"After lockdown, at three o'clock, I will get you a phone. Just ask your wife to send airtime to the number you are calling from."

Jan was about 50 years old and had spent most of his life in jail for a series of murders. He helped me with buying access to a bunk bed to sleep on and arranging calls. Within days I had my own phone.

Airtime and money transfer vouchers were the currency of prison – for buying drugs, weapons, cigarettes, even a bunk bed and protection.

I was beginning to understand the art of survival.

My top bunk was my haven, even if I stared into a fluorescent lamp just two feet above me, watching various insects navigating it. It was a place to escape, to avoid the glares or menacing gestures.

But there was also a thin veneer of order within the cell, perhaps because anarchy posited unimaginable horrors. The *huisbaas* organized the cleaning of the cell, which would be followed by bible study.

"Being locked up in a cell twenty-three hours a day with eighty other men is tough," Jan said. "But if you are tidy and thoughtful towards your cellmates it makes things easier."

"It's very important that you stand up for yourself; and you may have to fight if someone goes too far. You just have to let people know you will not be a bitch and are prepared to throw hands and feet when you need to."

I listened gratefully; he had form.

Bible study was fascinating. Suddenly, eighty men convicted or accused of all number of atrocious crimes would fall silent as one of the inmates began reading from the Bible. A couple of hymns would follow. It seemed like a brief oasis of purpose and belonging in a desert of futility.

But the desert stretched endlessly before me. Seven days

of this routine, these privations and the risk that Ullah Khan might get to me: I was desperate for news of my emergency bail application to the High Court.

My telephone calls with Munique were both treasured and painful. She told me that Chloe had asked if I had died. She relayed how supposed friends were avoiding her, how parents at Chloe's kindergarten steered their children the other way and never returned her calls about playdates. It didn't help that the local media had picked up my case, speculating wildly about who I might have defrauded, being fed a litany of lies by 'police sources.'

But my bail hearing would be Saturday; I might be out in less than 48 hours and could begin putting the record straight. Not an hour too soon; I was eating next to nothing, surviving on smuggled juice and cookies. My liver was still unhappier than the rest of me.

But my temporary attorney was going through the motions. The paperwork he filed was riddled with errors; he seemed insouciant about the whole process. But then he wasn't where I was.

In fact, he was a trickster. There was no emergency appeal, nor any weekend sitting. My brother investigated further – my 'lawyer' had in fact been struck off the bar.

Phone calls went unanswered and reality set in. I would have to wait the full week in jail. Every other day I was allowed two packs of cookies, four apples, one bag of tobacco, one pack of cigarettes, one take-away meal and reading material.

Such access to the wealth of the outside world helped me rise through the cell hierarchy. I was careful to share whatever largesse I had with the people who mattered, and especially Jan, who seemed the unofficial head of this prison wing.

Then there was Whitey, who had taken part in a gang rape while on some drug binge. Inside, and off the worst of the drugs, he was a different person.

Uncle James was in his 60s, convicted of rape but on the flimsiest of grounds. But who would leap to defend a man still addicted to meth, with not a cent to his name? He would probably die here.

Call it Stockholm Syndrome or similar, but I soon began to feel pity and sympathy for some (but by no means all) my fellow inmates. South Africa's jails, I concluded, were crowded with those most harmed or neglected by society, not populated by the people most harmful to society, like corrupt politicians. All but a handful of the inmates had grown up with an abusive father or without a father at all.

A week after arriving at Allandale, I was crushed into one of those airless stinking police vans for the reverse journey to court. Surely I would be free, in the clean open air, within hours. Schilz had nothing on me.

But he was giving a very good impression of having evidence of some sort.

My new attorney looked somber as I entered the courtroom. "More charges," he whispered.

I stood in disbelief.

At the other side of the courtroom, Schilz could scarcely contain his smug glee as he conferred behind cupped hands.

Another postponement: four more days at Allandale. I felt like the drowning man clinging to a rope as it is steadily lowered into the water.

I was escorted back to the holding cell, aware that my shuffling gait was similar to that of so many beaten inmates.

I slumped onto the concrete bench - my elbows on my knees and my head bowed down. And I had a conversation with God. Why was He keeping me here? What had I done? Did He have any sense of justice? On the walls, amid the scrawled profanities and gang symbols, someone had chalked *Jesus is the Answer.* At that moment I needed a lot of convincing. My hopes were evaporating fast. The lawyers wanted more money; my family seemed exhausted. But somehow the writing on the cell wall kept mulling in my head – *Jesus is the Answer.*

On my next call with Munique, she sensed I was shrouded in darkness, and took it upon herself to send me some Christian motivational books. She had always possessed a more genuine faith than me. I began reading one to Jan, who had never shown any interest in our daily Bible Study. He asked to borrow the book and disappeared to a corner of the cell, engrossed.

The following day – instead of leaving the cell during Bible Study to smoke some meth – he stayed. And he said he wanted to read from the book.

In halting tones, he recited the story of the donkey that had fallen into a pit. Unable to rescue it, the animal's owner decided to bury it and shoveled earth on top of it.

At first, when the donkey realized what was happening, he cried even more piteously. But then the wise animal hit on a plan. As each spadeful of dirt hit his back, the donkey would shake it off and take a step up on the growing mound of earth. Eventually, the mound grew high enough for him to jump out of the pit.

For some reason, I stood up next to Jan and told the other inmates: "Life is going to shovel dirt on you, but shake it off and take a step up. It will take patience and time, but we can all get out of the deepest pits by never giving up."

In truth, I had a supportive family, resources and education to help me clamber out of the pit. But as I looked at the other guys in the cell, I realized they had nothing.

CHAPTER EIGHTEEN

THE BLACK HOLE

Despite the return of my lawyer from his Spanish vacation, the bail hearings just got tougher. One was postponed because the magistrate's husband had died, which I thought at the time was very inconsiderate.

At the next the prosecutor assailed my character.

"Your honor, the defendant has proven himself a compulsive liar and cheat who has used his choir-boy face and smile to deceive and defraud," he began.

"He is without doubt a flight risk."

Schilz then claimed, based on a 'source', that Munique and I had already packed to leave when I was arrested.

So bizarre and dispiriting was the farrago of lies – all lapped up by a gullible media, that for a few days I began to see my prison cell as a refuge from the madness. From my top bunk, with my knees pressed against the ceiling, I could talk to Munique and Chloe, lose myself in books. One television set would be rotated between the cell block on different days and one particular Sunday, it was our turn to have the old box set. As Jan was fixing the receiver to get the best possible picture, an episode of Hillsong Church was broadcast. I remember Brian Houston's voice echo in the prison cell. "God has a plan for your life, all you have to do is give him a chance". That was a tipping moment in my life. I decided to leave everything in God's hands from thereon out.

And I felt, despite the privations, a strange sense of solidarity with the criminals that surrounded me in that cell 23 hours a day.

The bail hearing went on four days. No wonder there was a massive backlog of cases in the criminal courts. My defense team were confident I would be granted bail; they ought to be at that price.

So I had more than a few questions when the magistrate returned to court after lunch on day four to pronounce that "as the accused has not presented enough evidence on how his imprisonment will impede his personal life, I have decided not to grant bail."

With a casual knock of the gavel, he gave me a glance and swept out of the courtroom.

Father's Day was only a few days away and I would not be home. Chloe would be alone at the upcoming 'Bring Daddy to School' day, and everyone would know why.

An appeal to the High Court would take three weeks, my lawyer said. He was somewhere between apologetic and perplexed. I was somewhere between furious and desperate. I suddenly imagined being in that same cell for months.

Back at Allandale, I was waiting to be processed when another inmate – a member of the 28 Gang – started taunting me.

"Your wife's gonna find a new man; you going to be history," he smirked. Then leaning toward me, he added: "I hear she's already screwing somebody."

I grabbed him by his throat and slammed his meth-riddled body against the bars of the prison door, pushing his wasted frame as high as I could until he began to choke before letting him drop to the concrete floor.

You could hear a pin drop. The other inmates looked on. You didn't do that to a gang leader unless you were suicidal.

I told Jan about the incident as I dragged myself up onto my bunk. He went very quiet but began sharpening his metal spoon against the wall. But he wasn't the only one to be worried about my altercation with a member of the 28's.

The warden, a weasel of a man who had been the subject of a sex scandal involving a female prison employee, summoned me to his office.

He told me I was a trouble-maker, that I was disturbing the peace at Allandale. I wondered if Schilz had got to him. I was going to be transferred.

In my prevailing mood, I was in no mood to listen.

"The only reason why you are transferring me is because I am white," I snapped at him.

"It's because I get take-out meals, coffee, sugar and cigarettes, all within prison rules, and share them with my cell mates. And the 28's are jealous. I figured out your crooked system and exploited it to my benefit."

He made an odd snorting sound and waved me out of his office. Some of my cell-mates even organized a petition to protest my transfer. Perhaps they knew just how bad my next resting place was.

Old Malmesbury prison is just that: old. In prison, you never get a good night's sleep or a meal that resembles real food. Your status as a human being is revoked. People in uniforms think they rule you. They do whatever they want and get away with it.

The first thing you are ordered to do is to strip naked and bend over so that they can see if you are smuggling any contraband in your body cavities. There was no dignity. You are made to feel like an animal. There was a room full of naked strangers and I had to mostly detach yourself from my body.

I just knew prison life was about to get a lot more difficult. In this grim environment, humanity counts for little because to the prison staff, we really are just cattle: one on, one off and make a note of the numbers in and out. The prison cells reek of sweat, human waste, and filth with the stench of garbage hanging in the air.

I was frog-marched to a collective cell that made my old place in Allandale look like a hotel room. Suffocatingly hot, the narrow room had a stinking latrine, the only one still working, for its fifty inhabitants. The occupants were sleeping two to a bunk, top-to-tail.

Higher-ranking gang members, I guessed, got beds nearer the steel door – away from the overpowering stench of the toilet, where a multitude of flies congregated.

'I could die here,' I thought to myself. Nearly four weeks building relationships, gaming the system in Allandale, learning how to cope, had been discarded at the whim of a man who'd been caught having sex on the floor of his office. Now – once more – I had to learn who were the psychopaths, the addicts and the molesters.

I had managed to get a few 'luxuries' in Allandale, and a precious link to the outside world. Here, I had to squat next to the toilet to make a call in case the guards came past.

My first call to Munique was necessarily brief. I tried to make light of the transfer, said the place was much the same as Allandale. But she knew me well enough to detect that something had gone wrong, that the bleak had become wretched.

The guy who was running the cell was called Mabogey, a one eyed leader of the 26 Gang, who'd been awaiting trial for seven years for the murder of a family of four as part of a gang ritual.

'Seven years,' I thought, 'and his case has not even gone to trial. Could that happen to me?'

I was beginning to feel an emotional claustrophobia.

Twenty hours after I stepped into Old Malmesbury, a guard shouted my number, followed by the word 'Visit.' I was led from the cell to the visitation area, a tawdry place where you could only communicate through a dirty plastic screen.

I had no idea who had come to see me. My heart leapt just as my brain protested when Munique walked through the door of the visitors' area.

She loved me, she wanted to comfort me. That's what my heart told me. But look at me: dirty, disheveled, with a scruffy beard and eyes bulging from lack of sleep. Don't let her see me like this, my brain said.

She was accompanied by her mother, who had already done so much to raise funds for bail and pay lawyers.

Munique, a look of deep pain on her face, touched the screen with her slim, beautiful fingers. Which is when my self-control evaporated and I broke down in tears.

To be so close to her, but so stranded, unable to touch

her or even to hear her without pressing my head to the filthy screen – it was a form of torture. Made worse by the fact that my appearance would haunt her for hours after she left.

We were allowed only twenty minutes, and we had a crisis to deal with. Munique had sold furniture and other valuables to pay legal fees; the lawyers wanted more before they'd work on an appeal against refusal of bail.

Worse than that, Munique told me that Chloe was becoming very withdrawn, not taking part at school, constantly asking where I was.

I could handle the financial problems, address them rationally. But the thought of Chloe, at four years old, awake at night worrying about her Dad, sent me to a new low. A visit from my mother, who was clearly appalled by my appearance and predicament, did nothing to improve my spirits. I felt as if I was a burden and embarrassment to my family. And yet all I was, was a political plaything.

I thought of the parable about the donkey, and about how Jan had changed. But it all seemed so remote and irrelevant now; I did not have the willpower to climb out of any pit, however fine my words at Allandale might have been.

Deprived of a phone, I successfully begged for time to use the one pay-phone in the wing to call Munique.

It was by now early July. This saga, brought about by the malevolent Schiltz, had been going on nearly two months. And Munique had reached breaking point too.

"Things are not going well, Barry. We just don't know where to get the funds for this new set of lawyers, then there is still bail to be paid, if you win the appeal."

"Then, your new lawyer spoke with my dad and said you could be facing a good ten years in prison."

She sounded beyond tired, bereft of hope.

"I've already sold everything we possibly can, plus I pawned my wedding ring."

"Then there's Chloe," she said hesitantly, torn between my needing to know and the likely effect on my mental health.

"The school emailed me. They say she is going through severe trauma. She cries non-stop; she's angry, resentful."

Munique simply unburdened herself. I knew I had little time so tried to reassure her that I was doing fine.

"I'll see you soon; things will be better," I said. But the tears were already rolling down my cheeks. I didn't believe what I was saying; and nor did Munique.

Before I could say goodbye, the time on the pay-phone expired. Munique's voice was replaced by a steady monotone, as if mocking me in my humiliation.

At that very instant, I met the essence of despair; it crowded out rational thought or logic. Sheer emotion had taken over. My new found faith was hanging on a thread, or lost.

I returned to the cell and took out the pack of antibiotics I still had for my laryngitis, as well as the paracetamol for my liver pain.

I moved around the cell asking discreetly for one or two paracetamol from each individual. Soon I had thirty tablets.

I went to the basin and began swallowing every pill, one by one, careful to pretend that I was feeling sick. Even in despair, there was some cunning left.

I went to my shared bunk, hoping I would just go to sleep

and never wake up. My loneliness and isolation, my impossible surroundings, the suffering of my family – all of it would go away.

I dozed amid waves of nausea and heartburn, willing the medication to send me into a deep slumber. But it never did; and I shall never know why not. Had I fallen asleep, my body would have just shut down. Instead, the physical pain only grew.

I was groaning audibly and one of my cell-mates called a guard.

"The white dude is sick," he said. "Think he took a bunch of pills."

The guard would not have cared one iota had I had appendicitis, but a suicide attempt was different. He had a duty to act.

An Emergency Services Team arrived with foot and hand shackles that might have come out of a medieval jail. I had to shuffle in six-inch increments to a truck that took me to the nearest hospital. By now severe stomach cramps made me feel as if my spleen was about to burst; I was so light-headed I expected to fall over with every step.

I had to wait in line at the public hospital, attracting some suspicious glances as I slumped against the wall in my shackles.

My guards stood over me. One of them was a short, wiry black man with bloodshot eyes, who looked as though he had seen plenty of suffering.

He watched me, my vacant expression. And then he spoke, in an almost poetic voice, his rich baritone cutting through the ambient racket of the reception area.

"God loves you and He doesn't want you to go now."

I was jerked out of my catatonic state.

"God has plans for you. Don't do this again. Ask for repentance. From a short black man to a tall white man," he smiled, "let me tell you that there is life after darkness. I was a lost soul once."

They are words I can hear now. His words echoed that of Brian Houston back in Allandale.

*

Five hours later, I was surprised still to be alive. My guards lifted me up and led me to see a doctor overwhelmed by his workload. But he didn't get many shackled patients. I could tell, even in my dazed state, that he was wondering what I could possibly have done to have ended up in such a state.

"It's too late to pump out your stomach," he said. "So you'll be going on an IV drip and we'll do some toxicity tests, especially on your liver."

I was wheeled to the psychiatric ward at the other side of the hospital; I had, after all, just tried to kill myself. Behind an enormous steel door was a room stripped of anything a patient could use to harm himself or others.

I was attached to a barrage of IV drips and went to sleep; my first full night of sleep in seven weeks.

Thankfully, the next morning my liver count was still abnormal; there was still a great deal of paracetamol coursing through my bloodstream. I say thankfully because it meant I had to stay in the austere hospital room rather than return to Old Malmesbury.

And the prison governor had even arranged for a visit from

Munique and Chloe. Had the system suddenly taken pity on me? Or did he just not want an enquiry into the prisoner who tried to kill himself?

Munique was both horrified that I had taken so many pills, even though I painted it as an attempt to get sent to hospital rather than the morgue.

I tried to reassure her that I would never have taken my own life. And now, clinging to her hand for the first time in nearly two months, I could not believe I had reached such a nadir.

Chloe was shocked by my appearance and my beard, and couldn't understand why the 'two men' would not leave the room. At least they had been kind enough to remove my shackles and handcuffs before my wife and daughter arrived. Perhaps she would decide I was recovering in hospital.

Even though physically I was still something of a ruin, I gained strength from their visit. I would need it.

The day I returned to prison, there was a brawl between rival gangs in the food line. Blood ran across the tables and floor. There was no respite from the violence and squalor of prison life, nor from the gnawing fear of what might befall your loved ones on the outside. I was powerless in the face of both dangers. And they came soon enough.

Munique had been briefly fortified by her hospital visit, only to receive a call from my brother.

He had been threatened by the Pakistani crew and told that if a substantial sum was not paid to a certain disgruntled party, my wife and child would be murdered and they would arrange for me to be raped in prison. The 'enforcer' even found my brother and showed him photographs – apparently taken by a private detective he had hired – of Munique and Chloe.

I was distraught and furious. I wanted to break the prison bars with my own hands and use those same hands to kill the 'enforcer.' But I had to focus: my appeal in the High Court was imminent. If I could get out, I could help resolve the problems threatening to submerge my family.

A huge storm woke me on the morning of my appeal. The skies outside scarcely grew lighter with the dawn, so leaden were the clouds.

I muttered a quiet prayer to myself. This was conceivably the most important day of my life; there was no higher court to petition should my bid for bail fail. But I also prayed for strength should I be kept in prison.

I was not allowed to attend the hearing, but my brother and mother were there.

*

"Have you ever been inside an awaiting trial prison, Mr. Agulhas?"

The inquisitor was Judge Denis Davies.

The prosecutor, taken aback by the line of questioning, simply stuttered: "No your Honor."

"Well I've been there."

Judge Davies glanced at Colonel Schilz – whose complacent bearing clearly annoyed him.

With barely concealed contempt, Davies continued.

"Is this Colonel Schilz the only witness you called in the whole bail application, and whose testimony you rely on?"

"Yes, your Honor."

There were a few moments silence as the judge studied some papers in front of him.

He cleared his throat.

"Considering the arguments placed before me, I will be releasing the accused on bail. The parties can decide the terms and meet me in chambers for the final order."

I was a lucky man, not to have won bail but to have had my hearing adjudicated by Judge Davies. An independent judge frequently critical of haphazard, incompetent and corrupt police conduct, he was clearly unimpressed by the quality of Schilz' evidence.

Schilz looked stunned and shot an accusing glance at the prosecutor, whose only offense was trying to make bricks without straw.

CHAPTER NINETEEN

TRUE FREEDOM

My case had received a lot of press attention, some of it hostile, much of it skeptical. My new-found religious faith was mocked as a gimmick; people I regarded as friends before my stint inside avoided me. And yet I had not been given the presumption of innocence along.

Doing any sort of business while awaiting trial for fraud was like trying to sell eau de cologne in a pig farm. Added to which, I had an ominous sense that Burj Boy's friends might pay me a visit again.

With legal fees outstanding, no employment and no savings, I had exchanged one form of purgatory for another. But at least I was with my family again – and I would strain every sinew to protect them, and provide them with a stable, secure life.

First I had to staunch the downward spiral: our cars were repossessed, eviction in our rental home followed. We said goodbye to our home – the only home the girls had ever known – and walked away with nothing. My restrictive bail conditions began to gnaw at me: I was quick to anger and slow to fall asleep despite my freedom from prison.

We ended up moving with my mother into a two-bedroom apartment just before Christmas. Feelings of despair and failure were waiting for me when I opened my eyes every morning. Was this all because of my mistakes? Had I been stupidly naïve? Had I underestimated just how remorseless my enemies could be, and just how fair-weather my friends?

New Year's Day 2016 brought with it a stark clarity and grim mood of determination. I was not going to be defeated. Munique's eyes were too often rimmed red with tears; my mother wore a permanent grimace of anxiety. The kids were unsettled.

I opened my contacts file and quickly crossed off those who I'd not seen for years and those who would not want to see me. There were plenty in the latter category. But there were a few names left in what might broadly be described as the intelligence fraternity.

One after another, I reached out to them. I was transparent about my situation and clear that no work was beneath me. If I had to stand on a street corner watching some low-life's apartment, that was fine.

Gradually I scraped enough money together to get us a place on the coast, away from the curious gazes and snide remarks of our Cape Town neighborhood. It was, literally and metaphorically, a breath of fresh air. The long walks on the beach and cliffs helped Munique and I step back from the immediate crisis and revisit our life together. The girls loved the sea, and the wind and sun conspired to envelop them in a natural exhaustion that improved their sleeping.

I worked when I could and watched the unfolding negotiations between the international community and Iran with intense interest. My work for the United States had – in its own small way - helped bring Iran to the negotiating table by interfering with the lives of prominent sanctions-busters, providing their phone numbers, email addresses and bank account details. It had allowed federal agencies to peer through the key-hole and discover a whole chamber of connections.

One evening in January, I began reading about the prisoner exchange between the US and Iran that accompanied the bigger negotiations. I had mixed feelings about the clemency offered to several Iranians who had been central to the Islamic Republic's sanctions-busting efforts. President Obama commuted the 78-month sentence of Arash Ghahreman, who had worked for Koorush Taherkhani. Prosecutors also moved to drop charges against Taherkhani, who was still living comfortably in Iran. Taherkhani had been accused in of using a Dubai front company to buy U.S.-made marine navigation equipment for use in Iran, in violation of sanctions.

I was led to believe by my US handlers that several government departments were not happy with the news of Taherkhani and Ghahreman's good fortune.

At least I felt relevant again. But my renewed vigor and focus had an altogether more hazardous goal: escaping South Africa while awaiting trial. It was time to escape the cyclical nightmare that had become our life. Schilz, backed by a politically motivated National Prosecuting Authority would otherwise haunt me for as long as they possible could.

Preparing for the next phase of his persecution of me, Schilz had me placed on a 'Movement Activation List' (MAL). Anytime I showed a passport to authorities, a simple scan would show that I was not permitted to leave the country.

Schilz had got one thing right. I was a flight risk. He'd got another very wrong – underestimating my determination to evade the list.

I still had a few friends and contacts in the intelligence world. A private plane leaving from an obscure airfield could avoid the usual formalities, especially if I could find one – just one – and a sympathetic Immigration officer.

There was one possibility, an officer in the Customs service with whom I had worked on the cocaine and cigarette smuggling conspiracies, and who had been as appalled as I had when his superiors passed on the chance to make some of the biggest busts in South African history. We had stayed in touch sporadically. Would he do me an unlikely and very risky favor, or would he alert the police that I was planning to leave the country?

I thought long and hard before calling. First, I had to explore his thoughts on my well-publicized and protracted bail hearings.

"Barry, didn't expect to hear from you," he said when I finally took the plunge and made the call.

"That guy Schilz must hate you. Can't believe he expended all that effort to keep you inside. No idea how you survived Old Malmesbury; I'd have done myself in after about 24 hours."

He was sympathetic; that much was clear. It was time to make the pitch.

"Can I meet you somewhere; it's too sensitive to talk about on the phone."

Two days later, we sat in an alcove of a coffee shop in Cape Town's business district.

"It's not good to be seen with you," he said – only half in jest. "I had to cover my tracks coming here."

I had rehearsed the pitch countless times while pacing the sitting room or looking into the bathroom mirror. I had to make him think I still had value, was still in the game despite everything.

I dropped a few heavy hints about my continuing work with the US government, especially in reviving my Iran contacts, though truth be told it was at best occasional after the disruption caused by my jail-time. I was also beginning to get involved in tracking Islamist extremism in South Africa for my friends at the embassy.

He was suitably impressed.

"Thing is," I continued, with an unforced look of melancholy, "I just can't work here with Schilz trying to ruin me. The toll on my family has been unbearable."

I slipped a photograph of the girls across the table.

"This is all I really care about," I continued, "my daughters and my wife. My wife has been humiliated and traumatized by the events of the last year, my elder daughter is constantly anxious."

There was a pause.

"They're lovely kids," he said.

"I need to get out. My friends in the intelligence circles can have a new, official, US passport issued and arrange a private charter from an airfield without a customs office. I just need that official stamp that allows me to leave the country."

"But you're on the MAL, right?" he said.

"Yes, like being in prison but on the outside," I grimaced.

"Well, I must be crazy," he said – leaning back and stretching his arms outwards, "but I'll stamp your passport. I can profess ignorance or negligence rather than complicity. I'm fed up with it all anyway. The corruption is epic; promotion is based on ass-licking. Maybe Uncle Sam will have some work for me too...."

"I'd be the first to recommend you," I said – meaning every word of it.

In the next few days I feverishly worked with my contacts to start the arrangements. But it would come at a price.

In the end they found an EU-based leasing firm that would put a Gulfstream on the tarmac in South Africa and then take me and my family to safety.

The negotiations went into great detail. There could be no stop-overs in states that might send me back to South Africa – just in case Colonel Schiltz had gone to the lengths of organizing an Interpol 'Red Notice.' We decided on two technical stop-overs in Africa before heading west across the Atlantic.

We arrived at the departure airport shortly before dawn. It was eerily quiet, but there on the apron was my passage to freedom, a gleaming US-registered Gulfstream.

We unloaded the few suitcases we were taking and clambered up the steps into the spacious interior – normally the preserve of corporate executives and film stars, not a family on the run.

The pilots greeted us amiably but didn't ask too many questions. Perhaps this was not the first time their Gulfstream had been used as a getaway and I was sure they have been briefed on their mission.

Within minutes the engines started up. These guys were on the clock. Much of a delay and they would exceed their maximum flying hours for the day.

I listened intently to the chatter between the pilots and control tower, alert to anything that might spell trouble.

The senior pilot contacted the tower.

"November 112 Whiskey Alpha, requesting clearance for take-off to Foxtrot November Lima Uniform," the airport code for Luanda in Angola, our first stop.

"Negative, November 112 Whiskey Alpha. You need to proceed to Foxtrot Alpha Charlie Tango for customs clearance before proceeding to Foxtrot November Lima Uniform."

Foxtrot Alpha Charlie Tango was Cape Town Airport. One glance at my passport there and Colonel Schiltz would be racing across the runway within a half-hour.

"Ma'am, a customs officer already stamped us out at our hotel; we have clearance for a direct routing to Foxtrot November Lima Uniform."

The pilot sounded exasperated and irritated. If only he knew the full stifling reach of the South African state.

"November One One Two Whiskey Alpha, please confirm where I can reach the customs official who cleared you for exit"

I stood at the threshold to the cockpit. In front of the pilots there was a dazzling array of monitors and dials, all illuminated in a glowing orange against the purple dawn beyond the window. The one I fixed my gaze upon showed the flight plan to Luanda.

The pilot turned to me.

"What's the number of your contact? We don't have long before we will be grounded."

"November One One Two Whiskey Alpha," the air traffic controller's voice crackled over the speaker. "We've requested written confirmation from the agent's office that the passengers and crew are allowed to depart SA without passing through Foxtrot Alpha Charlie Tango."

Written confirmation? At 5am? For a flight that didn't even exist? My plan seemed to be crumbling by the minute. Soon the flight time would exceed the pilots' maximum hours and we would have to abort the whole plan.

I imagined a squad of police cars led by Schilz surrounding the plane – a look of beaming satisfaction on his face. I imagined my Customs contact suddenly getting cold feet and either telling his superiors or simply ignoring my repeated calls to his cell phone.

My frantic thoughts, now bordering on panic, were interrupted by a call from the control tower. I only took in the response from one of the pilots.

"Ma'am, does that mean we have clearance to start our engines?" the First officer asked the air traffic controller.

"November One One Two Whiskey Alpha, you are cleared to start."

It was as if the gates of heaven had opened. The crew speedily went through the take-off checklist, the engines started spooling, the door was closed and the seatbelt light illuminated. I settled into the oversized leather chair and buckled up. The girls had already fallen asleep.

I stared out the window as we taxied down the runway, the sun about to rise above the picturesque mountain range.

"November One One Two Whiskey Alpha, you are cleared

for take-off."

The engines were placed on full throttle and we accelerated down the runway. It was a moment of intense bitter-sweet. I was finally escaping persecution, taking my family to a new start in a better place. But there is no place on earth more beautiful than South Africa, I thought, as the rising sun illuminated the stunning landscape. And down there – somewhere – my brother and his family were still asleep, and my father was buried, in a country I'd never see again and I tombstone I will never visit.

*

It had been eleven years since I had dropped out of college on an impulse that I could make it in the aviation business. There had been the best of times, and all too often the worst of times. My marriage had been tested to the limit, as had my endurance and faith. I had grown to question my judgment of others; my trust in humanity had been constantly corroded. But surviving the bad times, enduring and overcoming a tidal wave of doubt, had ultimately made me more resilient.

It is sometimes said that our personalities are already moulded before we are two years of age. The rest is just tinkering at the margins. I profoundly disagree with that. But it does take adversity – and plenty of it – to put us to the test. We can repent our sins and failings; we can change our ways. But first comes trust – the trust that we can be better. It's understandably hard to trust that life can be renewed, but with God's guidance I have no doubt that it's possible.

On our own, we'll remain our old selves until we die. Though we might want to become better men, we won't succeed. That's what's behind Paul's frustration in the New Testament: "For I do not understand my own actions. For I do not do what I want, but I do the very thing I hate." (Romans 7:15).

Once we were safe and met with officials after the flight, I renewed my acquaintance with some of the intelligence officials I had shared so much with in previous years.

And with their blessing, I began to reactivate some contacts in the Middle East after information was received that Fat Waz has moved operations to Raqqa, Syria in support of ISIS, which opened a whole new series of events.

As Ronald Reagan was fond of saying: "Trust but Verify."

EPILOGUE

Finally, out of prison, I can reflect on the time I spent there and answer some of the questions I had asked myself while inside. Why had I been through this hell? The shame. The guilt. The fear. The physical and emotional devastation. How can I keep the promise I made to God? The promise I made but didn't have the strength to keep until now.

With tears in my eyes, a racing heart and shaking hands, I've found myself on my knees in front of the Lord many times, trying to work this out.

One thing I take comfort from is that at the start of my nightmare, I was weak, but somewhere inside me I always knew that God is faithful and I had no doubt that He would provide. When you go through hardships and decide not to surrender, that's strength.

I now owe it to many people to set the record straight. There have been so many versions of the truth in the media. Many lies overlaid with truths and truths overlaid with lies.

I have been to a place of true suffering and in this place I have found true humility. True strength, and true freedom. I now have the strength to forgive those who have wronged me, to let go of my resentment and my anger. As an adult looking back I wish I could give advice to the younger me, who was, at times, back then ridden with insecurities about things that mattered and weighed heavy in the moment, but don't now. Since I can't send today's wisdom back to the adolescent me, I'm glad that at least I can record it here in my book, for my kids to read and for others to draw inspiration from.

If I could, I'd tell the adolescent me to forgive yourself for mistakes and move on wholeheartedly. Forgive others. Let go of animosity. Be the best person you can be and try to see the good in others and in every situation.

I'd tell the younger me that positivity is a mental discipline; like eating the right kinds of foods, you must apply the same discipline in your own mind, exercising choice and discretion to stay healthy. Be kind to others (kindness costs nothing). Be a good friend. Know money, outward appearances and material possessions are not the best predictor of character. Be careful with and recognize the value of money; it has power to create security and should never be wasted. Be open to innovation; to trials and errors as each process has its own intrinsic value.

I'd say that hard work and persistence will be noticed by someone and will be remembered by you in times of self-doubt. Nothing of value ever comes easy. Eventually you will be rewarded in some way for guts, determination and kindness. It is okay to fail.

As Beckett says – fail better; pick yourself back up and try again. Not everyone gets an award for everything they do, but this doesn't mean there isn't value in that doing.

I'd caution myself to respect others. Respect and listen to opinions as sometimes you can't see clearly until you are a little further down the road. Be honest with yourself even if it hurts. Tell others the truth as you see it. Walking away can be a strength as well as a weakness—use your power to end things, justly and thoughtfully. Also, believe in and stand up for yourself (especially as you get older); no one else will, and outward strength is both a product and function of the protection you afford your inner self.

I'd tell myself that as you grow older you will wonder what is truly important in life. The answer is you should aim to be psychologically strong. You need inner strength more than money, grades, sex or material possessions. When you truly fall in love, your lover will recognize your strength and be drawn to it, and you to theirs.

Lots of other things matter in life and in love, but nothing quite as much as inner strength, so take every opportunity to nurture yours. It is already there, even if you can't see it. You should challenge it and push it beyond limitation in every possible way you can imagine.

If the incarceration experience doesn't break your spirit, it changes you in a way that you lose many fears. You begin to realize that your life is not ruled by your ego and ambition and that it can end any day at any time. So why worry?

You learn that just like on the street, there is life in prison, and random people get there based on the jeopardy of the system. The prisons are filled by people who crossed the law, as well as by those who were incidentally and circumstantially picked and crushed by somebody else's agenda. On the other hand, as a vivid benefit, you become very much independent of material property and learn to appreciate very simple pleasures in life such as the sunlight and morning breeze.

In the end, to some extent, I am happy that this happened to me. It strengthened my understanding of what life is about.

Sometimes, our dreams are aborted, our hopes are dashed, and our destinies are destroyed. We don't know the reason for why things happen as they do and we become angry and depressed at the world, at God, at everyone.

We often grow up with an idea of what our life will look like when we are at a certain age, more often than not, it is a realistic image, and more often than not, life doesn't necessarily mirror the image we had for it. At that moment, we can feel inadequate, we can feel like a failure and we can feel that we failed to create the life we want or deserve, but if we take a closer look sometimes the magic is in the journey rather than the destination, it is in the lessons we learn along the way and the changes we have to go through to become the best versions of ourselves.

When your life doesn't turn out the way you wished for, it will humble you. It will make you a kinder person, a more sympathetic person, a wiser person, a stronger person, a less judgmental person, a deeper person. It will make you human.

You will learn that you can't be perfect and you never will be, you will learn that you will fail at things you thought you were good at, you will learn that you can be hard to love sometimes, you will learn that you have bipolar tendencies, you will learn that you cannot control your surroundings and you cannot make someone change or someone love you.

You will learn to accept your fate and stop trying to change it. You will learn that life will scar you, and it will hurt you but it will also surprise you-sometimes in a good way, and one day you will look back and be able to connect the dots, one day you will look back and make sense of all the confusion, one day you will surprise yourself when you look at the image you had for your life and realize that it doesn't resonate with you anymore and it doesn't matter.

As humans we like to be tested. It's why we like competition. It's why we like risk. It's often the excitement of uncertain outcomes that drives us to learn from failures and improve, in the hope of avoiding more. But the potential for failure must be real. And when it is real, we will sometimes fail.

It's easy to give up when everything goes against you, trying to hold on when so many people want to see you fail is one of the most difficult challenges you will face in your life. All of us struggle and go through hardships or bad seasons at some point in our life, but it is those hardships we have to endure to grow as individuals

We men are often just wrong about failure. It seems we've all decided that if we ever experience failure, we're then failures. I want to tell you that this is not true. Failure is integral to human life, the way God designed it.

Look at Abraham, Jacob, Moses, David, Peter— they all experienced failure, because they were mere humans. Mere humans fail. But, it's good that we do. While we may not like failure, facing it helps us realize our potential.

Reflecting back on all that happened, I think that humans in general learn to postpone happiness. We think that we will be happy when something in the future occurs. Or when someone else does something we think we want or need.

We're always looking ahead as if the happiness we seek is just out of reach. But, this is an illusion. Like the vision of water just up ahead that constantly evades the thirsty traveler in a desert. Life is now. It can't be postponed and if you ignore it or withdraw from it, it just rolls by without you.

As individuals, we are the ones actually responsible for our own happiness. Real, lasting happiness is not something that comes from other people, or from possessions, achievements or events, even if they are pleasant and nice to have.

Happiness is a choice; it comes from within. You are the person in the drivers' seat. If you are happy with yourself and have inner peace, then you have happiness. If you don't, you have the power to make a change.

It is never a good idea to postpone happiness, because if you want to postpone it, there is usually an underlying problem that needs to be dealt with. And now, not later.

There will always be challenges in life and sometimes these will threaten your happiness, but during trying times, it helps to remember how short life is and how similar life is to a game. If you think of life like it is a game, you gain perspective on how temporary any success or failure is, and how enjoyable mere participation is (or can be if you let it). After any game, there is always another way to win or move forward. You just have to be willing to try again. In every moment that fleets by, there is something beautiful, worthwhile, precious. The trick is not to expect too much from life, to set realistic goals and always remember to be kind to yourself.

What to do about corruption in South Africa is one of the most important questions of our time. We have inherited a legacy of corruption in South Africa, after the departure of Nelson Mandela, a man with leviathan strength of character and a great leader. South Africa's Mahatma Gandhi. We owe it to his memory to stamp out corruption successfully.

I've had the privilege of experiencing different cultures and systems of political accountability as a result of my work. I don't have any definitive answers about what we need to do to address corruption in South Africa, but one thing I've drawn from my experience of corruption is to notice the difference between a codified system of justice, with written rules and one that is based on upholding principles.

The former is so easy to circumvent whereas the later requires a corrupt individual to fool a person's intuition – a much harder feat to accomplish. I think we need to move closer to a principle – based system of political accountability in South Africa, and so instead of asking "did this person break any written rules?" we must ask "did this person uphold the principles they undertook to uphold?"

If we can ask the right questions, we can arrive at the right answers more quickly, and we can root out people who don't deserve to hold public office more effectively.

Nor should we ever stop asking questions about how we can achieve a more harmonious, corruption free system of governance in South Africa. I think future South African governments need to place the beating of corruption higher up on the agenda. The question of how to beat corruption must never just be asked. It needs to be investigated. Researched. Analyzed. Just like we search for a drug to cure disease, we must never stop searching for a cure for corruption in South African society.

I also want to say a little about kindness, learning and moving forward, but Bear Grylls says is better than I ever could in his book *Mud, Sweat & Tears*:

Savor the moments of sheer happiness like a precious jewel – they come unexpectedly and with an intoxicating thrill. But there will also be moments, of course, when everything is black – perhaps someone you love dearly may hurt or disappoint you and everything may seem too difficult or utterly pointless. But remember, always, that everything passes and nothing stays the same… and every day brings a new beginning, and nothing, however awful, is completely without hope. Kindness is one of the most important things in life and can mean so much. Try to never hurt those you love. We all make mistakes, and sometimes, terrible ones, but try not to hurt anyone for the sake of your own selfishness. Try to always think ahead and not backwards, but don't ever try to block out the past, because that is part of you and has made you what you are. But try, oh try, to learn a little from it.

I believe my story will encourage people, attract people and draw people in. I can be mocked, rebuked, argued with. I don't care. I stand with my testimony.

If God has saved you, if he has rescued you, you have a story to tell. A person with an experience is never at the mercy at a person with an argument.

The fact is Jesus has changed my life and I will tell my story, but my past is not your past. My story is not your story. You also have a past. You also have a story. We all have. Each one is different but we can all adapt and change. Dying spiritually and then resurrecting spiritually as a Christian is nothing short of a miracle. Here I am. Living proof.

It was C.S. Lewis who said that "pain is God's megaphone to rouse a deaf world."

During the desperate, dark, difficult and confusing times, we must cling to the belief that God can do the impossible.

Yet when we are in desperate or feel surrounded by darkness, when times are difficult and confusing – this is when it feels almost impossible to believe in the impossible.

People tell you to pray and believe in a miracle, but your circumstances are telling you to be wary and skeptical.

I want you to know that your difficulty serves a purpose. I want to encourage somebody who's got some difficulty going on, some difficulty that you can't control, that your problem will serve a purpose.

We immediately rush to say 'bad', 'good', 'hard', 'horrible', and 'unfair'- when God might just be letting you go to that hard place so that He can move in power and do the unimaginable.

By faith you can trust God for the power to get through what you're going through. By faith you won't just endure the pain, but you will get something powerful out of it.

In the darkest day of my life, when I went through something that I would have never even thought to be my worst nightmare, I chose to believe God & not just look at what was there, but hear what God was saying about it and how He wanted me to reach out to Him.

I didn't *lose* heart; I was able to *take* heart. He gave me strength in the midst of the battle of my life. I had an anchor for my soul.

He can do the same for you.

ACKNOWLEDGEMENTS

I undertook the writing of this book without fully realizing the complexity of such a project.

I would like to express my gratitude to the many people who saw me through this book; to all those who provided support, talked things over, read, wrote, offered comments, allowed me to quote their remarks and assisted in the editing, proofreading and design.

I am thankful to my wife, Munique, who is the most extraordinary person I have ever met. She is velvet coated steel.

Immeasurable thanks to my literary agent, Thomas Leong, who has been a counsellor, adviser, psychiatrist and friend.

I am owed deep gratitude to Tim Lister, who has taken up the opportunity to work with me on this manuscript after I sent him a one liner e-mail. He brought his in depth investigative journalism to the project, fact checking everything, reading through countless e-mails and sensitive documents, allocating his precious time, sometimes while travelling in war zones and other inhospitable areas, because he believed in this project as much as I did.

Countless thanks to Catherine McCabe, my one-woman army, an amazing lady with a style of her own, who believed in me from the start and did the work of three editors, late nights and early mornings, to get this book to a final product. It was all worth it!

For those I worked with at the Department of Homeland Security, Defense Criminal Investigative Service, CIA, Joint

Terrorism Task Force, Belgium Customs Intelligence and HMRC, thank you for the work that you do, day in and day out, often without any recognition.

I'd also like to thank Alexander von Ness, Stuart Bache and Donovan Fichardt, who all contributed to the cover design.

Most importantly, I would like to thank my family. My mother, brother and sisters who helped me through some very dark times. Special thanks to my mother-in-law who has always been there to lend a helping hand.

Special thanks for my legal teams, Anthony Pocheco (USA), Ben Matthewson and Cornelius Smit (South Africa)

To Zetta, thank you for always sticking it out with us.

Last but not least, I beg forgiveness of all those who have been with me over the course of the years and whose names I have failed to mention.

CPSIA information can be obtained
at www.ICGtesting.com
Printed in the USA
BVHW032034080119
537351BV00001B/1/P

.